10 Skills for Effective Business Communication

10 SKILLS

FOR

Effective

BUSINESS

COMMUNICATION

Practical Strategies from
the World's Greatest Leaders

JESSICA HIGGINS, JD, MBA, BB

TYCHO
PRESS

Cover Designer: William D. Mack
Interior Designer: Meg Woodcheke
Editor: Brian Hurley
Production Editor: Erum Khan
Cover photography: NATALIA61/Shutterstock
Cover Hand Lettering: Alyssa Nassner

ISBN: Print 978-1-64152-098-0 | eBook 978-1- 978-1-64152-099-7

This book is dedicated to my mentor,
Jason Korman, for teaching a data-driven, overeducated,
high-vocabulary girl how to communicate well to
actual humans. Thank you from the bottom of my heart.
Furthermore, I live for the moments when I see
any human living their best life. This book is
dedicated to your pursuit of doing exactly that.

Contents

Foreword

Communication is fleeting. We live in an age when it's impossible to absorb all the channels of communication that are swirling around us. That's why effective communication in business is more important than ever.

Over the past twenty years, as I helped hundreds of companies reach their full potential, I had to become an expert on corporate communication. I've seen the best and the worst of it—firsthand. It may seem strange that a dyslexic person would excel at business communications, but it's exactly because it did not come naturally that I had to overcome my weakness and understand every aspect.

I have worked with Jessica Higgins at multiple businesses for the last decade. I have seen how powerful and refined her communication skills are. Jessica combines several communication channels effectively to produce the results that her clients want.

Jessica and I sincerely believe great marketing is part of the DNA of any great business, and all great marketing comes down to communication. Whether it's written, verbal, online or with AI, communication means everything to you, and your business. For some people it's an inherent talent, but for every one of us it is a necessary skill.

Developing great communication skills has led me to great success in my life and my businesses, and I sincerely hope you will take the valuable lessons in Jessica's book and apply them to your daily work and life as well.

Cheers,
Ben Way

Introduction

Effective communication is the key to pretty much everything.
Besides being what separates us from the other animals, it's what
allows us to do important things like share ideas, learn, build, and
grow (and the less important things like post a grocery haul video on
YouTube, talk about what happened on the season finale of *Stranger
Things*, and write Yelp reviews).

And yet we "do" communication mindlessly. It's a habit. But for
most of us, it's a bad habit. Ineffective communication can accidentally start a war just as effective communication can end one. This
book examines exactly why, how, and when we should communicate.
For those of you looking to improve yourselves, this book is for you.

This book is equal parts research and practical advice. Think of it
as your modern guide for keeping out of trouble, influencing others,
and leading your team to greatness, whether that team is a *Fortune*
500 company or your family.

But before we get into how to communicate, let's start with
exactly why this book is for everyone. I am a corporate growth and
development expert with a background in research and a focus in
organizational culture. What I learned from working with top CEOs
and from midnight calls from friends in relationship disasters is that
communication is a problem for *everyone*. My intense research in
crafting meaningful communications taught me that communicating
is a skill. Because it's a skill, this means two things: (1) anyone can
develop it, and (2) it is not an innate human quality or a gift.

I am writing this book to share the most practical advice that has
come from my research in communication because I am on a mission
to help you communicate more effectively. Developing great communication skills requires focus, effort, and a willingness to learn. Don't
worry, you're going to fail. So let's accept that now and know that
failure is requisite to learning. We are all human. You will get better
over time.

This book will be your guide to learning effective methods of communication. If you practice over time, your life, your career, and your relationships will improve. This is my promise to you. Your promise at the beginning of this journey is to learn and practice. I'm going to take you up on your promise. Now let's get to it.

HOW TO USE THIS BOOK

This book is designed to be your definitive resource for practical business communication skills. It combines the concepts of many other works in the fields of communication, negotiation, body language, sales techniques, and human influence into a one-stop resource designed to give you the practical skills you need to know and master. You can read this book from beginning to end or skip around as you like. Each chapter provides a tool set of key skills for mastering an area of communication, as well as practical examples to help you practice and develop each skill.

If you're facing a real-life communication issue now, skip straight to the appendix (page 107). I've provided a chart for you that sequences the skills you need to develop across a set of business hypotheticals, from hiring someone new to public speaking to having a difficult conversation.

After reading the book, keep it handy and revisit chapters as they become relevant in your life so that you can continue your communication practice. Each chapter is designed to be a stand-alone guide for you to do exactly that. Some of the skills in this book may come naturally, and others may take lots of practice.

1

KEEP YOUR MOUTH SHUT

Listen more. Talk less. Be decisive.

—SATYA NADELLA, MICROSOFT CEO

Our team has worked with Microsoft for a very long time. Many years back, when Steve Ballmer was CEO, Microsoft's share price was in decline. Despite the company having many customers, it had only a few fans. Ballmer was great in a lot of ways, but I'm convinced he wasn't so great at listening. He was about pushing products within his company and to the public. He was focused on this cycle: design products, sell products, repeat.

What every bad communicator knows is that it doesn't matter how great your ideas, how perfectly eloquent your wording, or how polished your execution and delivery. If the person on the receiving end doesn't actually listen or doesn't care about what you're saying, you're finished.

This is the tricky part about communication. Being a great communicator isn't about you at all. It's about them, the recipients of the message. As my friend and colleague Brian Solis says, "Attention is a currency." You can't expect people to tune in automatically because your mouth opens. In fact, we have to get people to want to tune in to us.

How do you do this? Easily. You must master the art of open listening, of influential listening, and of capturing a message you can then use to make your communication resonate.

OPEN YOUR BRAIN AND KEEP IT OPEN

Our brains and our technologies are hardwired to work against us when it comes to listening. First, you have your heuristic brain patterns (see page 3) constantly seeking shortcuts to better understand information so that you can tune out and move on. You also have the brain networks that control your judgment. This area refuses to accept novel information, ideas, and people that don't fit comfortably into your current mental models. Add to that technology constantly pinging away at your attention span. Open listening comes from an open and focused mind. Clearly, you have a lot stacked against you. But don't worry, we are going to heighten your sense of awareness and practice self-restraint.

Truly listening to someone has become outmoded. This is a very good thing. Becoming a great listener is your surefire way to stand out, gain attention, and significantly increase your likelihood of crafting communications that resonate with the person you are speaking with.

The best way to learn how to listen is by learning how to avoid *not listening*, since listening itself is fairly straightforward. Following are the three main enemies to good listening. Shutting them off is your key to success. When you begin falling into one of these three traps, slap your brain out of it. After all, it's not in control here—you are.

Don't Formulate a Response, Ever

Becoming a great listener can be extremely difficult if you like talking a lot. We can't help ourselves—we want to jump in and add to the conversation. Well, now is the time to stop that for good. Each time your brain starts articulating a response as someone else is talking, give yourself a mental slap. Slap all of the nonsense out of your brain and keep it open to the words coming at you. Focus on those words.

Avoid Sentence-Grabbing and Sentence-Cutting

Want to make someone dislike you? Cut them off midsentence. Or even worse, hijack a word or phrase someone says and begin talking about that instead. It will veer the entire conversation into a different direction, thereby ensuring that you missed the message. Also, it will expose you for what you are: a jerk.

Every time we communicate, we are attempting to express a piece of ourselves in some way. Don't hijack someone's moment or cut them off at the knees. It's bad for you and them. Stop that thought. Slap it away and stay focused.

Shut Down Brain Biases, Judgments, and Conclusions

This is the trickiest habit to practice because you're going to have to recognize behaviors happening back in the mainframe computing sections of your brain. You probably don't even realize they are happening. In fact, there are hundreds of them and when they take over, your brain stops listening. The first set of programs are called heuristics: well-intentioned shortcuts our brains make to produce a judgment. Then there are biases, which are shortcuts our brains take to jump straight to a conclusion without hearing all of the information. The following is an exercise for shutting those programs off, which must be done if we are to become great listeners.

Suspend Your Beliefs

Imagine that you're listening to someone speak—someone you don't particularly like. You hear them make an inflammatory political statement that pretty much pisses you off.

It was actually the moment you decided that you don't like them that your brain began filtering information. Your brain stopped listening. Even worse, you heard an inflammatory statement. When that happened, your brain launched a full mental filter that further blocked you from listening. These filters are designed to focus only on the information that confirms your beliefs. Most everything else gets lost. What now? Brain-slap time. Suspend your beliefs for the sake of listening.

The best come prepared, meaning that it's worth the mental effort to work through your own biases about a person, or an idea, or a thing, before you hear them. Decide that you are going to suspend your beliefs. In the concepts of emotional self-management, we call this deconditioning a trigger. You know when you get triggered. Now know that whether you respond, shut down, or don't react, it is at least partly within your control.

INFLUENTIAL LISTENING

Unfortunately, all listening is not created equal. There's the type of listening that makes people want to work with you, the type that makes people hate you, and the spectrum in between. In this section, we are going to learn how to master the art of the right type of influential listening.

In everyday life, most people default into treating listening as an act of silence. However, why waste such an excellent opportunity to influence the speaker when it's your turn to speak? Listening with influence involves activating good body language and avoiding distractions.

Eye Contact, Facial Expressions, and "Stop Looking at Your Phone for One Damn Second"

Eye contact is an essential body language technique for listening because it both improves your ability to listen and signals to the speaker that they are important. By eye contact, I don't mean staring at the person the entire time, as that can get a bit creepy—but aim for at least 80 to 90 percent eye contact. That is, when someone is speaking, try to hold eye contact with them 80 to 90 percent of the time. You'll notice with practice that you become a far better listener through this simple trick alone.

Wearables

I once saw a corporate executive smoothly check his smartwatch throughout a meeting without anyone else in the room even noticing. Wearables and other seamless technologies like them can assist you here if you have the type of job (or significant other) that requires your constant attention. Proceed at your own risk and be smooth about it.

As a person whose face shows my feelings, I'm pretty terrible at this skill. However, when it comes to good listening, your face must be inviting for the other person to want to speak, or the whole exercise becomes futile. Check in with your face when someone speaks. Feel for your face muscles and soften those muscles. Parting your teeth slightly is a common trick that yogis use to practice facial relaxation and create mental calm. In addition to improving your focus, this will help you act and look like a better listener. Whether you're nervous, scared, or downright pissed, keep your face soft and open (just like your brain, dear listener).

Perception is reality. The majority of us have an overconfidence bias when it comes to skills. We think we are above average drivers and that we can effectively multitask. Unfortunately, all the research shows that multitasking is a lie we tell ourselves. Put down your damn phone and keep it down until the end of the conversation. Show people you are committed to them and their message.

FINDING MEANING IN THE MESSAGE

Finally, active listening is a search for meaning. Don't just listen to the words, seek to understand what the speaker truly means. Getting to the root cause of someone's words is where listening transforms into powerful communication. Listening involves dialogue, done correctly. Once someone has spoken, whether it's your boss, your social media followers, or a particularly unpleasant coworker, dive in.

Want to benefit further from listening? Research shows that when managers listen to employees for six hours per week, it boosts employee engagement by 30 percent, improves inspiration in employees' work by 29 percent, and boosts innovation by 16 percent. This means that implementing and practicing great listening skills in your business can boost emotional and financial gains from your workforce.

How Listening Is a Lesson in Communication, from Microsoft's CEO

I chose Satya Nadella's quote to open this chapter because watching him lead Microsoft taught me (and I'm sure many others) an important lesson about the power of listening. Satya hit the Refresh button on Microsoft's strategic direction in 2014, revamping one of the world's largest technology companies by first listening to his audience and then taking action. And he did it by being an excellent communicator. Satya listened to what his customers, his employees, and technology users were saying. He then spoke to them with an open letter on day one as CEO, and he kept speaking to them. This changed the game drastically for 50,000 Microsofties, and it was just the beginning.

Satya Nadella's e-mail to employees on first day as CEO. As published on February 4, 2014, by Microsoft News Center.

From: Satya Nadella
To: All Employees
Date: Feb. 4, 2014
Subject: RE: Satya Nadella – Microsoft's New CEO

As we look forward, we must zero in on what Microsoft can uniquely contribute to the world. The opportunity ahead will require us to reimagine a lot of what we have done in the past for a mobile and cloud-first world, and do new things.

We are the only ones who can harness the power of software and deliver it through devices and services that truly empower every individual and every organization. We are the only company with history and continued focus in building platforms and ecosystems that create broad opportunity . . .

This starts with clarity of purpose and sense of mission that will lead us to imagine the impossible and deliver it. We need to prioritize innovation that is centered on our core value of empowering users and organizations to "do more." We have picked a set of high-value activities as part of our One Microsoft strategy. And with every service and device launch going forward we need to bring more innovation to bear around these scenarios.

Next, every one of us needs to do our best work, lead and help drive cultural change. We sometimes underestimate what we each can do to make things happen and overestimate what others need to do to move us forward. We must change this.

Finally, I truly believe that each of us must find meaning in our work. The best work happens when you know that it's not just work, but something that will improve other people's lives. This is the opportunity that drives each of us at this company . . .

Satya

Ask Open Questions

According to a 2016 article published by *Harvard Business Review*, Harvard University researchers found that people who are perceived as excellent listeners had one significant difference in their approach: they ask a certain type of question. They ask questions that are open and designed to help the other person better understand the topic of the conversation. The more deeply you can understand the speaker, the easier it becomes to craft your communication to them. This can be done in a business meeting or even over Instagram. Keep the questions limited to ones that require a long response, not just a yes or no.

Avoid Leading Questions

In the same Harvard study I mentioned previously, bad listeners were the ones who grabbed on to a piece of information and led it in a different direction. Remember to avoid this type of conversation hijacking. Focus on the topic while it's going. Listening is an act of patience.

Search for the Why Behind the Words

Our primary goal as communicators is not to be the ones moving our mouths the most or using the fanciest words. It is to connect people to a message. To do this, we must know what they want and then craft our language to give them a version of it. That's what great communication does. Which is exactly why listening is the first communication skill we are reviewing. Sometimes people simply want to be heard. Other times, they want to persuade. But why is that? Seek out the *why* behind the person talking.

Ask and Ye Shall Receive

Ask open questions that build on the conversation. They can be as simple as, "Can you tell me more about _____?" or, "Can you give me an example?" or, "What led you to believe this?" Well-crafted open questions invite your speaker to dive deeper into the conversation. This will give you better listening skills and a better understanding of your listener and their message.

KEY CONCEPTS

- Clear your brain
- Listen for the purpose of actually listening and not responding
- Never cut off the speaker during a sentence
- Don't hijack a mentioned thought
- Stay on topic
- Maintain eye contact
- Practice Zen-like awareness of your facial expressions
- Listen free of technological distractions
- Ask open questions that seek deeper meaning
- Avoid leading questions
- Seek to understand your speaker

ASK YOURSELF

Listening is a key skill to every chapter in this book. In the next conversation you have, stop your mind from wandering or forming a sentence. Ask yourself: "Am I listening? Am I adding to the topic we're discussing? Am I maintaining eye contact and good body language? Am I not looking at my phone or getting distracted?" My friend and colleague, Cameron Herold, recently told me he sits on his hands when he's listening to remind himself to be an open listener. Whether you physically or mentally cue yourself in, check on your listening skills each time you communicate until it becomes second nature.

2

THE SECRET CODE
OF BODY LANGUAGE

_Although our body language governs the way other
people perceive us, our body language also governs
how we perceive ourselves and how those perceptions
become reinforced through our own behavior,
our interactions, and even our physiology._

—**AMY CUDDY**, PSYCHOLOGIST AND TED SPEAKER

Carly Fiorina and Hillary Clinton were both case studies for body language during our last presidential election. They were scrutinized as appearing too cold, stiff, and unlikeable. Their body language was attributed to them losing the 2016 presidential election, which isn't far off base. In fact, undergraduates at Harvard were shown tapes of unknown gubernatorial candidates and could predict the winner with incredible accuracy, just based on the candidates' body language alone. Here's another strange statistic about body language: We've all heard the disparities between men and women in the workplace. Women are paid less, given fewer promotions, and receive more criticism in performance reviews than men. But here's one rarely published bit of research, according to Carol Kinsey Goman: Women who can turn on and off their assertiveness at will are far more likely to get raises and promotions than both men and other women. Skillfully showing endearing body language at certain times and portraying dominance at other times can make women statistically *more* successful. The following skills can be mastered by anyone, so don't worry.

This chapter will explain how to utilize body language to your advantage to become more confident, win friends, and spot phonies. It will also outline when and how to use these skills in business and social settings.

CONFIDENCE 101

Let's begin with the large vertebral structure holding you upright. Outside of signaling whether you've fallen or fallen to sleep, your spine has lots to say. The goal is knowing how to say the right thing, at the right time. It starts in your spine. When someone walks into a room confidently, they're easy to spot. Same with low-confidence people. Notice the spinal differences at your next networking event. It's all about the posture, baby.

There are two common body language tricks inside the public speaking circuit: (1) the superhero stance and (2) the winner's *V*. Both body language moves are designed to prepare you to be more confident when you need it. Do either in private right before you go on stage. Your stage can be a big negotiation, a difficult talk with your partner, or any event where a little added confidence is needed. These two tools are your body language hacks for winning. Both increase your body's confidence-boosting chemicals and help trick yourself and your audience into believing that you are in fact a winner and a hero.

Creating Body Confidence

The winner's *V* was discovered by a team of researchers who studied people throughout the world right after winning a big event. They found that winning has a universal sign language. Whether you are running an Olympic marathon or capturing your dinner in a remote jungle village, all winners from around the world display the same body language: they stand up tall and throw their arms up into a strong, high *V* shape.

What's even more interesting is that researchers found you don't actually have to win at anything to receive the benefits of winning. Standing tall and putting your hands up into this position tricks your body into believing that you have won. Serotonin and testosterone levels rise and your body begins to carry itself more confidently right after.

Think of this as your espresso shot of confidence. When you need it, sneak off to a private place and hold your hands up high, standing tall, and count to 10 seconds. The longer the better, but this is the minimum.

Imagine me standing in a bathroom stall before my executive strategy meetings doing this. It happens. Your body can't help but smile and walk itself with greater pride afterward, so pay no mind to the silly feelings you get during this exercise. I use this body hack when I need a shot of happy, confident chemicals to my brain right before standing in front of large audiences. Do it right before your event if you can.

How to Express Your Confidence

You should always be as confident as possible. Less confident people make far less money, ask for fewer raises and promotions, and get passed over all the time. This is as true in nightclubs as it is in the workplace. The body language you must absolutely stop projecting today is shoulders slumped, arms crossed. If you make yourself appear smaller, you will make yourself feel smaller. If you can't help but hunch over a computer all day, remember to take a moment to stop, spread your shoulders back, and make yourself feel larger in the room. The same rules apply to networking events. If you look around any networking event, the least social people will physically appear smallest: hunched over, arms tucked into themselves, legs crossed or otherwise together. Pay attention to your own body language with scrutiny. A large open stance will boost your morale over time and make you more comfortable in even the most awkward social settings.

Superhero Stance

Chapter 7 is dedicated to assertiveness, so add the superhero stance as the necessary first step to your more assertive communication style. Amy Cuddy's team of researchers found that when they forced college students to hold dominant poses, the students behaved with significantly greater dominance, asserting themselves to a far greater extent than their peers. This dominance shot will improve your confidence and boost your ability to assert yourself. Do it right before you communicate, if you can.

Here's how it works: Stand up tall and imagine that you are Batman or Wonder Woman after a hard day's work of being rich while ethically fighting off evil villains all night. Assume the position: hands on hips, shoulders back, chest proud, and chin up.

Ignoring the fact that you are, again, doing strange things inside a bathroom stall, hold this pose for at least 10 seconds. It is guaranteed to increase your testosterone levels and give you confidence caffeine. Researchers have proven time and time again that our bodies respond positively.

WIN PEOPLE OVER AND SPOT FAKES

Persuading others and identifying phonies is the hardest of all body language techniques and requires a fair amount of skill and practice. For an in-depth analysis of body language mastery, pick up a copy of the book *The Definitive Book of Body Language*. For now, we're going to cover the body language moves that have the greatest net impact on your business and relationships.

Learn Your Face

We all know how and when to smile and to frown, but only trained professionals are clear on the third type of facial body language: no expression at all. This is an extremely effective approach to controlling whatever room you are in. There is nothing that tweaks a recipient faster than showing no facial expression whatsoever. If you're in a situation where you want to make the other person feel uncomfortable, put on your poker face and drop all facial expressions. Give them no reaction whatsoever.

This is a common practice in hiring and recruiting. Good human resources professionals are trained to test how applicants react under pressure. It doesn't require any verbalization whatsoever. They simply sit, without reaction, and let you talk. Remember this next time you find yourself babbling. It's your body's response to seeking approval from your peer. Now that you understand this, rest easy with new-found self-control in knowing that this is simply a trick, and you're wise to it.

The Art of Becoming a Mime

If your goal is to win someone over quickly, mimicry is a great hack that doesn't require speaking. Clustered mimicry techniques amplify your pair-bonding with someone instantly. By *clustered,* I mean you must employ three or more techniques in a single interaction. A single expression may not get noticed, but research shows that three is the magic number for effectiveness.

You do this by adopting a similar facial expression to someone you want to instantly develop a closer relationship with. If that person speaks when they smile, well, so do you. If they speak with sternness, then do the same. Notice their hand gestures: Do they use large motions or none at all? Take this approach when it's your turn to talk. How is the person standing? Slightly alter your stance to match. Mimicry is all about similar body language and similar actions and reactions. With a little practice, you can create a kindred spirit in your recipient, without them even noticing.

Use Body Language to Spot Phonies

We might be able to control our words, but most of us never take the time to control our body language. When a person you're communicating with is saying one thing, but their body language is sending a different message, this is your red flag that something is awry. For instance, when a person says to you that they are great but their shoulders are slumped, you just know something isn't quite right. This is one of the reasons body language is so incredibly important. It not only allows you to communicate better, but it can also make you more charismatic.

All people want to feel that they are known. The art of charisma is about making others feel that you know them and you want to know more. If you notice that a person's body language is arguing with their words, simply call them out. Employing the open question techniques from chapter 1 (page 8) is a great way of accomplishing this.

In a simple setting, you see someone slumped over with unconfident language, but with words they express that all is well. Simply ask them, "Everything okay?" And then truly listen. Talk through work, life, whatever is going on. So long as the person is willing to open up to you, you've just won over a friend. See the following sidebar for a master class in taking this one step further and making someone change their body language.

There are more complex settings where bad body language happens, especially in business. Like when you are giving a big presentation to a room and someone's body language is sending

Body Language Master Class

Once you practice and become comfortable with the basics, it is possible, if you desire, to control others' body language as well as your own. This requires a high proficiency in smooth body language techniques. Be sure to practice them to perfection or you risk coming off a little crazy with these master steps. The secret to controlling the body language of others is to fill the room, take on mimicry, and then start moving your own body differently. If done well, the other person will move their body, too.

EXAMPLE 1: You start a conversation. The other person's arms are folded. Now your arms are folded. You move through the conversation, nodding when they nod. When you can feel them catching on, break your body language. Unfold your arms and grab your drink. They will grab theirs. Now replace your body language with the open and dominant poses you've just learned. Your recipient is likely to play along. It shouldn't be perfect symmetry. That would be weird. But when you like, start the flow again of body mimicry and changing body language.

EXAMPLE 2: The techniques in example 1 can work in group settings as well. If you're giving a presentation and everyone is seated, seat yourself. As you go through your presentation, connect with each individual through eye contact, a bit of body mimicry, and proceed like this randomly through the room. Then, when it's time for something important, break your body language and show deep interest. Lean in closely or even stand up. Embrace a dominant pose. You will own the room and others can't help but take notice.

I strongly suggest you practice each of these techniques thoroughly, as good body language is crucial to becoming the skilled communicator you are meant to be.

you bad vibes. Calling them out works especially well here. Simply ask, "Dan, is everything okay?" This opens up the opportunity for meaningful dialogue that can get you to your desired goal. It's always better to be in the room when someone is talking about you. Think back to high school–gossip days. Position yourself to defend, not to be taken when you're missing from action.

KEY CONCEPTS

- Take on a winning stance to instantly boost your self-confidence
- Master facial expression control to win friends and trip up your enemies
- Clustered body language miming will win you new friends
- Pay attention to incongruences between words and actions to spot and win over phonies
- Employ mimicry and then change body language to control the room

ASK YOURSELF

My hope is that you feel as confident as you can. Before your next meeting or presentation, step aside and ask yourself: "Am I feeling my most confident? Have I assumed a power pose?" Do not tread lightly, friends. A power pose is the difference between success and failure. Assume yours.

Also, the next time you want to make a friend or win someone over, ask yourself: "What body gestures do they tend to show?" Assume those. To become a master, get into a flow with your audience. Ask yourself how that person moves and move like them. Become a mime, not overtly but with slight moves. Watch and learn what slight moves you can make. The less overt, the better.

3

PRACTICE EMPATHY

Empathy begins with understanding life from another person's perspective. Nobody has an objective experience of reality. It's all through our own individual prisms.

—**STERLING K. BROWN,** EMMY AWARD–WINNING ACTOR

T

his chapter is all about empathy. We know that becoming an empathetic communicator is key to becoming a compelling communicator. But why?

This can be best explained with a story about my idol, Ray Kurzweil. If data scientists were given the same clout as rock stars are today, Kurzweil would be David Bowie. He massively contributes to the field of technology and artificial intelligence. He hacked human life with a supplement regimen that can change your body's chemistry and allow you to live longer, or so he claims. He even predicted and has hypothesized about the point at which humans and artificial intelligence become one (known as the singularity, which he claims is happening in 2045). His daily e-mail keeps science fans up-to-date on the future of robotics, computing, health, and human life.

I had to meet the guy.

And I finally did, at a talk he gave at Singularity University, a computer skills campus he cofounded on abandoned NASA property. Kurzweil walked in and began talking. He talked about his childhood, his school performance, his accolades, and his companies. He talked, and talked, and talked—only about himself.

We all sat quietly, politely listening to Kurzweil repeat his own Wikipedia page. We already knew all this stuff. We wanted something, anything insightful. When he stopped talking he left the room immediately, without shaking a single hand. The room was depressed. You could hear mutters. None of them were positive.

Having snuck into this thing for free, I felt for everyone else. They had paid thousands of dollars for an hour of nothing. Kurzweil didn't seem to mind at all. It was hard to leave without feeling disappointed or hating the guy. Empathy is the glue that connects us to others. Without it, we are merely selfish assholes.

EMPATHY IS A SKILL: PRACTICE AND DEVELOP IT

Empathy is an incredibly useful skill for becoming an effective communicator. It's easy to confuse empathy with sympathy, so let's disambiguate what empathy isn't. Sympathy happens when you are able to share a feeling. You see someone sad and you also feel sad. Empathy goes beyond that. It happens when you are able to put yourself into someone else's shoes and imagine and even predict their experiences. Practicing your empathy skills requires a bit of imagination, but don't worry—it's a fun exercise.

Next time you're out and about, select a random person to focus on for your empathy training. For instance, let's try it with some grumpy, yoga pants–wearing mother in a grocery store. Walk with her through her day. You wake up early and immediately become the short-order chef to an entire, and probably unappreciative, family. You don't have time for coffee. You have to feed, wrangle, and clothe your children to avoid arrest for negligent parenting. You manage to throw on yoga pants, despite *not* getting to attend an actual yoga class. You pack your animal children into your bus-size vehicle and drive to a school. Feel frustrated yet?

Practice your empathy skills daily, preferably with people you don't particularly like. It will make interactions smoother and less stressful, because you can relate more deeply to their human experiences and communicate more deeply as well. Developing an empathetic mind-set reduces tension and stress when you are confronted with difficult people. With enough practice, you can stop reacting to anger, craziness, and other difficult situations altogether. Empathy practice makes it obvious that we're all just human and we're all just doing our best.

Put Empathy into Action with Design Thinking

In business, moving from an empathetic mind-set to empathetic behavior is called design thinking. Seems a little counterintuitive that design thinking is all about action, but that's business jargon for you. Design thinking is all about focusing on people, not on tasks, technology, or anything else. It's about gaining a deep understanding of people and their needs, then designing for those needs. This sounds pretty basic, but it's easy to get offtrack. When we're building a product, we can get lost on the specifications. When we're writing a novel, we can get stuck in the ideas. Design thinking is mostly about self-awareness. Always remember your target audience and stop yourself before you go astray. If you do run off on a tangent, revert back to your end user. *What do they want and need?*

Design thinking can apply to improving communication, building better products, or anything else you want to accomplish. When someone's needs are met, they will feel more connected to you as well. The point of empathy is the same: to connect with and meet another person's needs. And this is exactly what great communication is all about. Meeting a need can be as simple as teaching a lesson, providing new insight into a thought, or presenting a new idea. There are six principles of persuasion, according to Robert Cialdini, author of *Influence: The Psychology of Persuasion.* This means there are six basic ways for you to influence people's needs. They are (1) reciprocity, (2) scarcity, (3) authority, (4) consistency, (5) liking, and (6) consensus. To briefly explain, people like to match gifts with gifts; they are more likely to be interested in something scarce; they trust authority figures; they will behave how they have behaved in the past; they like saying yes more than no; and they like agreeing with the group.

What this means is that you must first understand a need to be met in someone. Then, approach it with persuasive techniques; for example, reciprocity. If you want something, give something. You'll get something back. Design a way for the group to agree and the person you need to agree will be more likely to do so as well. There are many ways to practice design thinking and empathy in work and other areas of life.

HOW TO SHORTCUT EMPATHY IN DAILY WORK AND LIFE

Think of empathy as reverse engineering your brain. Whenever you communicate, it is vital that you understand that communication isn't about you. Yes, you are delivering the words, but your relationship with the message must end there. It's about the other person or people you are delivering the words to. Whatever the point you want to get across, reverse engineer it. Make it all about the listener.

When empathy is employed, communicating becomes easy. By meeting a need in people, you can influence them to make nearly any decision. This type of influence is very powerful. First, we are going to listen to, connect with, and hop into the shoes of your intended audience. Next, understand their needs and meet them. Sound taxing? It is. *Harvard Business Review* refers to empathy as a bottomless pit of energy depletion. It will be mentally draining for a while, at least until you get good at it. When the wheels start cranking on autopilot, it will all be worthwhile. My point is: keep going.

Putting Empathetic Communications into Action

When humans speak, they can't help but leave breadcrumbs for understanding more deeply. Listen carefully, then search for these clues. Not only hear them. Hear the *why* behind the words.

Search for clues to understanding the speaker's purpose, then craft your messages to them in order to meet that purpose. Remember that the goal is to meet with and deliver on a need here. The next time you meet someone new, try it out. Conversely, hear their message, and then define the topic. If this were a television show, would it be a family drama or a talk show? Was the person talking about themselves a lot? Were they trying to convince you of their prestige? Our words are a passage to the inner workings of our souls and communicating is our attempt to let people get to know who we are, in some form or another. This means that no matter how tightly someone holds on to their hand in poker, empathy will give you a sneak peek at their cards.

For instance, a person who speaks in terms of family, their children, and their community is a collective, familial type who values consensus and alignment. A person who speaks disruptively is exactly the opposite. They value freedom and perspective. There are many different types out there who all value different things. There are plenty of psychological profiling tests you can take to learn about the topic. However, I find most of those personality tests to be like horoscopes: universally applicable, oversimplified, and minimally useful. Following is my personal, biased chart to understanding human psychology when it comes to communicating with influence.

COMMUNICATING WITH EMPATHY

Personal Opinions

If you hear a lot of . . .
"I" statements and "My opinion is . . ." and you notice they aren't afraid to express themselves and their personal opinions more than their peers . . .

It tells you that . . .
This person desires influence, acknowledgment, and confirmation of their own genius. They want to be correct. They want to be the creator of brilliant ideas.

And you can craft your message like so . . .
Form your communication as a question or series of questions that leads them to believe they created your idea themselves. Start by asking, "Have you ever thought about . . .?" and gently lead them down your desired path. If you can create the impression that your idea was theirs all along, they will own and drive it for you.

Multilateral Thinking

If you hear a lot of...
"We" and "us" statements and you notice them soliciting the group's opinion before, or in place of, making a decision alone ...

It tells you that...
This person likes consensus and dislikes disruptors. They want decisions to be agreed on by everyone before they are enacted. Pose your communication to the crowd as an open question. Guide everyone to the right answer (yours) and make it feel like a group decision.

And you can craft your message like so...
If you're talking to one person, you could say, "What would you and your friends or family think about ...?" and guide the collective decision that way. You'll get your way by community vote.

Judgment Statements

If you hear a lot of...
Judgments about other people and comparisons to others (especially in a derogatory sense) ...

It tells you that...
This person feels threatened by others and desires feelings of security, belonging, and even superiority.

And you can craft your message like so...
Any message that builds the ego works well here. Craft your message with, "We both know you're brilliant. I'm sure you've already thought of ...?" Test out your version for the least condescending delivery method possible. This can be difficult to achieve.

Praise

If you hear a lot of...
Frequent compliments and acknowledgments of other people (e.g., accolades and positive statements) ...

It tells you that . . .

This person desires that others are pleased and happy.

And you can craft your message like so . . .

Make your communication fun, engaging, and a team sport. Turn it into a game that everyone can play.

Big Ideas

If you hear a lot of . . .

Mentions of big ideas, cutting-edge research, findings, and experiences . . .

It tells you that . . .

This person values a learning and growth mind-set. They will be open to new ideas and open to challenging them.

And you can craft your message like so . . .

Pose your idea as thoroughly researched as possible, then prepare yourself for battle. Be ready to answer tough questions. Don't be scared, the right answer will win in the end.

The preceding examples are basic psychological profiles to help guide you, but this doesn't have to be so complicated. Empathy in practice can be as simple as finding a common interest and sharing it. If you both like basketball, utilize the language and connection around it to form a deeper connection. Find shared experiences, hobbies, or even goals.

Become Your Own Devil's Advocate

Crafting more empathetic communication can come from simply debating yourself. Put yourself in your opponent's shoes. It's hard to side against yourself, but play through what a dissident rebel would say in response to your words. Then play back to *why* they said it. Roll the tape all the way backward. Where did the reasoning and opinion originate? If you can land it correctly, it can help improve the crafting process for your communication altogether, creating an improved version of what you are trying to express.

The deepest form of instant connection can happen when you share common values. If you notice that someone, like you, values safety, make them feel safe. If they value money, make them feel that they will be rich. If they value meaning, well, give it to them. Listen and then give people a vision of what they want—with your message in mind. Your words, crafted with a beautiful bow, make your target audience immediately interested.

Does this sound like manipulation to you? It should, because it is.

COMPANIES ARE OBSESSED WITH EMPATHY THESE DAYS

The term *empathy* has replaced *culture* as the one of the most common business buzzwords used today. Business leaders ask our team to design more empathetic corporate cultures at a quickly increasing rate.

Business journals have defined empathy as a huge competitive advantage for teamwork, innovation, and delivering better products and services to customers. Millennial generations are reported to be more empathetic and there is a presumption that more empathy from leaders will facilitate greater connection to millennial workforces. This is absolutely true if you consider that empathy simply facilitates connections between people. The problem is no one knows how to magically create empathy. Telling your employee to be empathetic is like telling someone to have trust: it's pretty oblique. Empathy is largely subjective inside organizations and it is a mystery to employ.

Business leaders are tackling the task of empathy by pasting it into the core-values document and even hiring for empathy traits. However, empathy is a skill, so that's not quite right. The truth with any organizational culture is that you can bring skills into the company, but they can be lost or gained once inside your company's true culture. Despite the difficulty in finding it, a more empathetic workplace truly is a better one. All of our research and design work shows that it leads to more creative work, which is on the rise in this country as we move from a manual labor workforce to one of digital and creative labor.

Here's How to Employ Empathy in Your Business

If you would like to spread empathy inside your organization, it can be achieved by simply breaking down the actual behaviors you would like to see, much like I have done for you previously. Then, lead with those behaviors. Spread and socialize them with your friends. Reinforce them daily. While there is no universal guide to organizational empathy, I will provide a few steps for you to take that will foster a more empathetic work culture:

- Design for empathetic behaviors that collectively meet your company's business outcomes and that are supported in your organization's work structures
- Drive continuous learning initiatives throughout your organization to foster creative thinking and outside-of-the-box connections
- Promote cross-silo and cross-departmental opportunities for collaboration to improve interpersonal empathy across physical spaces and cultural groups
- Develop curiosity programs, out side-of-work learning opportunities, and unexpected skills trainings and courses
- Promote title-free zones and reduce perceived authority biases (this will cut through barriers to empathy between job levels and titles)

- Empathy is about sharing in someone else's experience; it is beyond just sharing a feeling
- Practice empathy by imagining others' experiences
- Put empathy into action by designing for your end user
- Empathy becomes influence when you connect with and meet someone's need
- Empathy can be used to strengthen your own arguments by becoming your own devil's advocate
- Empathy becomes part of a culture when its core behaviors are modeled and reinforced

ASK YOURSELF

When new ideas and behaviors are reinforced throughout a culture, it becomes the culture. By this, I mean that behavioral norms dictate what is right and what is wrong to do. For the same reason you don't curse in church, the strong behavioral patterns you develop in your organization become the norm within that organization. Constantly ask yourself questions that will keep your behavior and ideas on the right path. There are things we simply do and do not do.

4

PSYCHOLOGICAL COMMUNICATION AND OTHER LANGUAGE HACKS

Words are, of course, the most powerful drug used by mankind.

—**RUDYARD KIPLING,** 19TH-CENTURY NOVELIST

In my very first consulting engagement, I remember the COO of BURGER KING® saying to me at one point, "I've told people this a million times." I remember it so well because since then it has been the one universally common statement in all my consulting projects. Every leader at some point will say, "I've told them over and over again and they just aren't listening." It's so funny to me every time because if a problem is somehow everyone else's and you are the exception, then it actually *is* your problem, as a general rule.

You can say things to people a million times. The issue isn't always *them* not listening; in fact, most often it is you not communicating correctly. Great communication is the linchpin skill of the best leaders of all time—from Abraham Lincoln to Martin Luther King, Jr. to Apple's advertising agency, TBWA\CHIAT\DAY. Communication is the number one reason that couples end up in counseling. If only we could drag our bosses or our subordinates to couples counseling as well.

UNDERSTAND COMMUNICATION BRAIN ERRORS

Computers are perfect communication machines. They minimize, if not eliminate, errors. You type code into your computer and it simply registers. Human brains, on the other hand, maintain a network and variety of shades for every single word we use. It's what makes our brains the creative geniuses they are. The word *autumn* not only takes on the basic meaning for us but also evokes the color of leaves or the taste of pumpkin chai latte. Quantum physicists in the artificial-intelligence field are attempting to tackle this computer weakness with big data. A computer simply registers the word *autumn*. It has no understanding of anything outside the context of that simple word, meaning that communicating with a computer today is actually pretty damn boring. While our brains are autoconnecting shades of meaning to each word in amazing ways, this also leaves many opportunities for coding errors.

Two people in the exact same room can register two words completely differently. Now add a hundred additional people and you've got yourself a coding error of infinite proportions, for every single word. As a skilled practitioner of communication, the first step in communicating is understanding that between you and any other person is two layers of coding, which often produce errors. Your job is to reduce and eliminate these errors. Furthermore, look for them. When a miscommunication occurs, don't take it personally. Our brains are merely trying their best. We are not computers; we are just people.

Keep It Simple

There is a standing norm in business that complexity is somehow serving communication well. It may make you feel safe, smart, and even fancy, but this is a fallacy. Brilliant leaders are those who can communicate ideas as simply as possible. Writers for national newspapers have a rule that they must write at a fifth grade reading level. This ensures that people actually understand what's being communicated. Unless your goal is to confuse people, keep communication simple.

It also helps to communicate to your audience. Give them only the nuggets they need to know and that they care about. The large amount of information that got you where you are currently is meaningless unless your customers need more information. If that's the case, leave the heavy information behind in a written case study or research report for their additional reading. This can show that you have authority while keeping everyone in the room on the same page. Keep the communication in the room simple. Give people exactly what they need to know.

Here's a concrete example to further solidify the point. The following is a communication I found published online:

Our mission is to become the market leader in providing business communication services at affordable prices, including VoIP, fax, analytics, virtual conferencing, and customer management products. Our vision is to become your #1 choice for serving all of your business communication needs. Our primary objective is to reach this goal through creating powerful, simple, user-friendly products with the highest level of reliability, and providing what we call "Amazing Service®."

Don't bother rereading it six more times to get the point—I'll help you out:

~~*Our mission is to become the market leader in providing business communication services at affordable prices, including VoIP, fax, analytics, virtual conferencing, and customer management products. Our vision is to become*~~ *your #1 choice for serving all of your business communication needs.* Our primary objective ~~is to~~ *reach this goal through creating* ~~powerful, simple,~~ *user-friendly products with the highest level of* reliability, *and providing what we call "Amazing Service®."*

A fifth grade English version so you can actually get the point here:

We strive to be your #1 choice for all of your business communication needs. We will win you over with our powerful, simple products and we will deliver the highest level of Amazing Service® to you, every single day.

Make sense now? Once you remove all the technical jargon and speak directly to people, it just makes things easier. Notice that I took the word *reliability* down to more specific, sticky language: *every single day*. I took *"Our primary objective"* down to the user level: *We will win you over.* Don't waste time talking about you when you could be talking to someone else.

Business terminology simply isn't necessary for great communicators. Speak to your audience at a level they can understand and appreciate. They don't need specifications or objectives. All that stuff may have meaning to you, but check back to the previous chapters: this isn't about you. Give your audience a reason to care. Audiences care about their needs. Speak to those. Leave the old language back in those Management 101 textbooks.

You can practice this concept by writing out your words, then revisiting them with a sharp knife. Cut out everything superfluous and whittle down the technical jargon to simple language. Reducing coding errors and reducing confusion are what make for great communication.

Practicing Real-Life Mind Control

There is one particularly peculiar area of interest in the world of psychology and communication. It involves the effects that stories have on our minds. Humans have passed along stories since we first began talking. Generation after generation, there is a set of stories we all hold deeply. They teach us lessons—they teach us about life and people. No one has ever passed a pie chart along to their kids. This is because our brains literally love stories. We hold on to them more deeply than any other form of narrative. Researchers found that when their subjects were told stories, they could retain the information five times longer than by any other means of communication. When they began looking into why exactly this is, they found that our bodies release oxytocin, or "happy" chemicals, when we hear stories, which solidifies them more deeply in our brains by associating stronger chemicals with the stories.

The research goes much further than this. Liu et al. studied brains firing on fMRI machines. It should be little surprise that two different brains tend to fire differently. However, when one person tells a story and the other listens, their brains begin lighting up the same. Boom. Welcome to mind control.

If there is a piece of information you would like to transmit, weave it into a storytelling narrative. Excellent storytelling can take years to master. (Our company released an e-book with LinkedIn that's free to download on the Internet, if you would like more information. It is called *Once Upon a Digital Time*. In it, we dive deep into the art of storytelling.)

HERO'S JOURNEY

The basic principles of a good story are pretty straightforward. From Homer to Miguel de Cervantes to George Lucas, great storytellers throughout the generations have followed a pretty specific format. It's called the hero's journey.

You set up your protagonist. Please note that (especially if this is for the purposes of business) your protagonist should not be you. Make it a customer or someone related or relatable to your audience. That protagonist then experiences a problem or hardship, which they must set out to overcome. The protagonist is not Superman. He or she experiences failures and shortcomings along the way, which teach us lessons. This can be based in your research and findings to help get your point across. The protagonist ultimately overcomes the struggle and how they do so is the lesson in our story.

I know this sounds a bit oblique, so here's a concrete example from our work with a pharmaceutical company: A mother discovered that her son had severe ADHD and needed medicine. She sought available drugs for him, only to discover that they all left him with no appetite. He stopped eating. While his ADHD had subsided, he became malnourished. Worried for her son, she knew there had to be another way to help him that wouldn't stunt his growth during these crucial years. She wanted him to grow up tall and healthy like all the other kids. During her research she discovered that transdermal medication delivered through an arm patch rather than a pill gave him the steady dose of the drug he needed to stay focused in school, but because it did so slowly, he didn't experience loss of appetite. Thankfully, he began eating again, studying harder in school, and we are so grateful to have helped develop the transdermal delivery system that allowed this one kid to live a healthy life and have a healthy future. Think of how many kids just like him are being helped. That is the power of transdermal delivery. And this is only one application.

See how I did that? Take your message and craft it in a way that allows your reader or listener to go on the journey with you. It will solidify all of the heightened emotions you need to make your communication memorable. It's a way to create communications that truly stick. And isn't that the point?

WHEN IT'S OKAY TO USE EMOJIS, IF IT'S EVER OKAY

There are only two universal languages that exist in the world today: (1) numbers and (2) emojis. Every single human across our Earth can understand a smiley face, a sad face, and even a winking face. Think about the power of this for a second. There are so few ways to cut across cultures and language barriers, why wouldn't we take advantage of emojis?

In Praise of Emojis

A very influential business executive and client once sent me a beer mug emoji after a long day. There's no way to interpret that as incompetent—I absolutely shared the sentiment. Emojis can help us connect to each other more deeply as humans. They let us share feelings.

Old-school, conservative business folks may tell you that emojis are never appropriate in the office because older generations don't understand them. Well, here's the truth: We're all human. Everyone has a Facebook account and everyone knows what an emoji is these days. Protecting older generations from emojis is no different than protecting millennials from hard work. It's simply ageism. Let's put it to rest already.

In 2017, a group of researchers found that sending emojis in work e-mails makes you appear less competent. This story went viral in the media and emojis became the official faux pas of office life. Then, productivity applications became common at work, with nearly all of them using emojis to communicate more efficiently and effectively inside the office. They're back.

This section is aimed at setting the record straight, once and for all, for exactly when and how to use our international language of emotion. The emoji can be a powerful thing. It can also be downright annoying. Use emojis over text, digital communication (including social media and even e-mail), and whenever communicating a feeling is necessary to the sentence. For example, an interoffice work e-mail that says, "Great work on that project, I'm so happy" or, "Great work on that project 😊" is perfectly fine.

An emoji will express that you are incompetent if you use it superfluously. No different than writing *very* next to every word in your e-mail, superfluous emoting sends a generally incompetent vibe. For example, an office e-mail that says, "I'm so very happy to talk to you. I'm very excited for us to catch up," comes off just as poorly as, "I'm happy to talk to you. 😊"

Do you see the difference? Emojis and other emotive expressions can add to a sentence or completely diminish its power. Emojis can connect us to each other's feelings when they are expressed simply as that: feelings. It is achievable to maintain your serious stature in the workplace while also being a human who does, in fact, smile. Sending each other emojis like this can even connect us more deeply.

KEY CONCEPTS

- Our brains naturally produce coding errors when we communicate; our goal is to reduce these errors so we all understand and share the same message
- Keep communication simple and make it about the end user
- Avoid complex, technical jargon; if a fifth-grader can't understand you, try again
- Stories resonate far more deeply and should be used for messages that are important
- Emojis can be a human-centered, universal communication system when used to express feelings
- Don't use language or emojis superfluously; keep your words concise

ASK YOURSELF

When you're ready to language-hack, ask yourself the following: "Am I making this as easy and simple as possible? Can I tell a meaningful story here? Finally, is it acceptable to use emojis here?" You will be surprised at your answers.

5

NETWORK YOUR WAY INTO ANYTHING

A good leader doesn't get stuck behind a desk.

—**RICHARD BRANSON,** INVESTOR, ENTREPRENEUR, AND PHILANTHROPIST

Tony Hsieh once taught me the most powerful lesson of my entire career: that the difference between becoming a great CEO, versus everybody else, is being in the right place at the right time and taking advantage of the opportunity. Don't get me wrong, he is one of the most brilliant people you could ever be in a room with, but his lesson resonates with me because of all the other brilliant people you could also be in a room with. In all of my work with great leaders around the world, I have always asked myself: "Why them? I know so many smart people who accomplish so little. How have these few really set themselves apart?"

The truth is it's all about who you know. Once you get in the right room, then it's just about spotting the opportunity. If you've ever read Tony's book, *Delivering Happiness*, you know that he was the owner of venture capital firm Venture Frogs when he took on a part-time role at a company named Zappos. He then took over as CEO and grew one of the most culture-centric businesses of all time, selling off to Amazon and then using the cash to reinvigorate downtown Las Vegas. If it weren't for him being in that right place at that right time, he could easily be just another Silicon Valley venture capital guy. Instead, he's the mastermind behind an entire city and company.

This chapter is about networking your way into opportunities.

For most people just getting started, networking events end up feeling a lot like a high school dance. You show up, hang out in a corner with your friends, and afterward think about all of the missed opportunities and people you could have spoken to.

COME PREPARED

The best come well prepared. Find an attendees list for your event or ask for one. Log into LinkedIn and find faces to match the names. Do a little research to get a better understanding of interesting people you may want to meet. The best communication happens long before the event. Come up with key topics to discuss when you meet someone for the first time. For even better preparation, pick up local journals and magazines to see where people you want to meet are hanging out. If you notice important faces at an annual gala, use your time and energy wisely by heading there rather than the countless other options available every Tuesday evening.

Whether it's a major event or a mixer, don't walk in cold. My coworkers and I make this an established practice. If you're going to take the time to walk into a room, take the time to find some people you would like to meet beforehand. This gives you something to do and makes it easier to open up conversation. You already know a few key facts about the person so you aren't cold-calling on them to enter into a discussion. When making your introduction, it's perfectly fine to let the person know that you know who they are and that you want to meet them. This makes people feel important. People like to feel important.

Bye, Bob

Here's an example from a recent health care conference I attended:

"Excuse me, I believe your name is <JANE DOE>. You're the director of patient care at <HOSPITAL>. I wanted to come introduce myself to you because I am excited to meet you. I love the work you did with _____."

An example of a bad introduction would be the opposite of this:

"Hi, my name is Bob. I work in finance. I love dogs."

One version makes the other person feel special. The other makes them feel downright bored. Prepare yourself well and people will appreciate the time and effort you put in. That's a pretty good start when it comes to connecting.

Timing and Positioning Skills

Reduce the social urge to walk in late. In a business setting, late is always unfashionable. Arriving early gives you a smaller pool of people to converse with, which means that you're more likely to get a deeper connection. It is my personal rule to always leave happy hours or other more social events early, as nothing gets accomplished in the last hour of drinking because not much gets remembered. Stay until the end if you like, but there is no reason to. As for where to position yourself, you don't need a real position. Stay open to others, wander about, and casually look for the people you may already know or consult the list of people you would like to meet. The goal is to appear friendly and open, not lost or closed off. Practice by entering a networking event early and stopping at the door. Take a moment to scan the room. There is no need to dash in or run for the bar. Assess your surroundings for a moment. It will help you feel more confident once in the room.

HOW TO CONNECT WITH STRANGERS

If you find yourself in a place with no familiar faces, don't freak out. Just remember that we're all awkward humans, stuck in a room together. You can get through this by staying calm, being prepared, and remembering these next steps.

A common misstep in networking is the spray-and-prey approach: connecting with as many people as possible, exchanging as many cards as possible. I recently watched a man shuffle through an entire event in 20 minutes, simply introducing himself and handing out business cards. Complete waste of cardstock. *Would you call that guy?* No. Talking to strangers is actually pretty easy in a networking setting, with these three previous concepts: listen (chapter 1), ask open questions (chapter 1), and practice empathy (chapter 3).

American culture can be pretty harsh. You get defined by so many factors: what you do for work, what type of car you drive, who you know. It's an endless merry-go-round of trying to "out fancy" each other. Networking events can feel like this times a thousand—rapid-sequence introductions and rattling off our job titles. That's why we hate networking so much. No one likes feeling judged. Or worse, no one likes feeling used. This is the innocent by-product of someone asking you, "What do you do?" at a networking event. It's the euphemistic question for, "What can you do for me?"

Using Business Cards

Business cards have an interesting history, dating back to the 15th century. They started as calling cards for announcing the presence of an important guest. By the 17th century, they were given to doormen to formally announce the name of the person arriving. Shortly thereafter, they turned into tiny advertisements that people used. It all pretty much went downhill from there.

A general rule for exchanging business cards is that you shouldn't do it unless you are going to follow up. There is no worse feeling to a person than giving you a card and having you ghost them. Simply don't do it.

Opening Lines

To be an extremely effective networker, you must be an effective connector. It's all about practicing empathy, listening, and asking open questions. Avoid sounding like everyone else—stand out with these opening lines:

"Hi there, I don't know anyone here. I wanted to come say hello."

"Why did you decide to come to this?"

"What do you do for fun outside of work?"

Flow with the conversation, actively listen, and share experiences. It's that simple, so long as you don't ask for anything or want anything more than a simple exchange of information at the end.

If you choose to exchange business cards, that's totally your choice. We are in the digital age of communication, after all. If the exchange is appropriate, trading e-mails with your smartphones is a much friendlier and connective approach. It can make you feel like actual friends. It also makes it easier to follow up the next day.

This is simply all business cards are meant to do for you: trigger you to follow up the next day, which you must absolutely, always do.

TRANSACTING BUSINESS AFTER THE NETWORKING

There is a point at which your networking efforts translate into business; it's just much further along than you think.

Your follow-up after a networking event should ideally contain the following three elements:

1. An effective reminder of who you are;
2. A piece of value or help that you can provide for them, even if small;
3. A specific time and date at which the next meeting should occur.

Notice that at no point have I pitched any products or services. Effective follow-up is about minimizing the transactional nature of the relationship and maximizing the interpersonal side. People will do business with people that they like, respect, and trust. E-mailing someone a piece of marketing material is equivalent to posting it on a billboard outside your house. No one cares. Building relationships is about building care.

If you can offer value in some way, even as small as introducing a new restaurant, and ask for nothing in return, you will absolutely get a response. Even if the person is too busy for lunch, you will get a response. In a sea of ignored e-mails and missed connections, this approach holds high value. During the first, second, or even third meeting, the opportunity to do business together will naturally arise. By the point that it happens organically, the answer is likely yes.

Become a Digital Networking Pro

Networking online can be even more effective than face-to-face these days. You have the same opportunities to foster a deep connection and aren't limited to the people in the room. People are constantly telling their stories online. Don't just hit the Like button. Comment, message, and interact. Dive into conversation with someone from the convenience of wherever you happen to be in the moment. If a person you wish to facilitate a connection with posts a photo of their dog, ask their name in the comments. Everyone loves attention online.

Share a Passion

An extremely good networker recently met me at a conference where I was speaking, added me on Instagram, and then reached out in direct-messaging to ask more about my passion for cryotherapy. This instantly solidified an ephemeral connection and I guarantee you that next time I see him I will surely go say hello. Yes, I know that he wants to do business together and he's the type of person I will absolutely be primed to do business with. He showed that he cared and it matters.

Practice your online skills by asking to connect with people you meet on Instagram, Facebook, or LinkedIn at the end of a good conversation. Take a screenshot of their profile and then find a way to connect at a later time. Don't make it superpersonal or invasive—simply inquire about a passion or interest.

One of my clients is a major executive at LinkedIn. Had it not been for his social media profile, our relationship would purely be transactional, but thanks to social media I discovered his love for rock music. Now that we share stories online about great concerts, it's a lot easier to get a response when I need something from him at work.

Putting It All Together

Here's an example of the preceding points employed well:

"It was a pleasure to meet you last night. I really enjoyed chatting with a fellow foodie. I would love to hear more about your actual business as well and I was just thinking, there is a great new lunch place near your office named ____. Would you like to meet for lunch this Thursday or Friday at 12 p.m.? If that doesn't work for you, send me some alternate times."

KEY CONCEPTS

- Your only goal for networking is to simply connect with people
- Prepare by studying the audience beforehand
- When you walk into the room, take a moment before diving into networking
- Arrive on time and leave early or on time
- Listening, asking open questions, and empathizing are the keys to turning strangers into connections
- Exchange information however you like
- Follow up with value and business will eventually follow
- Embrace social media and use it to conveniently solidify and deepen human connections

ASK YOURSELF

Please, get out there and network. And when you do, ask yourself: "Have I looked up a few people I particularly want to know online beforehand? Am I able to arrive on time?" And during the networking event, be sure you are asking open questions. Afterward, always follow up online and via e-mail. Finally, there's no need to wait for an upcoming event. Go digital. Connect with and direct-message people you want to know. It takes time to build a network, but trust me, it's worthwhile.

6

HOW TO GIVE AND RECEIVE CRITICISM

We all need people who will give us feedback.
That's how we improve.

—**BILL GATES,** ENTREPRENEUR AND PHILANTHROPIST

46

The world of corporate culture contains all sorts of radical ideas from all kinds of companies. One of these companies is Bridgewater Associates, a global investment firm that preaches the principles of radical transparency to all of its employees. In shorthand, if you don't speak the absolute truth twice, you're fired. This is touted as a culture-centric business model. A friend worked there as a researcher and described to me a culture of such brutal bullying that she quit after a few weeks of near sobbing. Radical feedback may be a business model for investment-fund types, but for most of us, it can be pretty uncomfortable.

The opposite of this is the standard approach preached in business books, which I call the compliment sandwich: "You're great, but you're behind on deadlines, but you're great, really." Most of us see through this nonsense. Let's work on skills that display genuine transparency in communication. We don't have to take an extreme company-wide approach, we just have to adapt some skills that work for all.

RALLY FOR THE PERSON

We are all familiar with the metaphors of carrots and sticks—rewards and punishments. Too much punishment makes people numb to harshness and criticism. Too much praise makes them soft to reality. Just like good parenting or healthy living, remember that everyone needs balance. It's good for them.

When it's time to have a tough conversation, context and framing is everything. Remind the person why you care and are bothering to discuss whatever the topic may be. For instance, "I believe in your talent and what you are capable of. I believe you are the type of person who values continuously improving and I want to work with you on this." When people are framed with *why* you're bothering to give feedback, it changes the dynamic of the conversation to open them up to receiving it. Otherwise, you may be speaking to closed ears.

Make Feedback Specific and Actionable

Have you ever stopped to notice how telling someone "great job" isn't very valuable? I mean, yes, it feels good, but what does it actually mean? Why did I do a good job? Specific details and actionable steps would be valuable in letting me know how I can do it again, thank you. When it's time to give less-than-great news, vagueness can be frustrating. This is why it's crucial to give feedback that is both specific and actionable. Your goal is to make this interaction as valuable as possible, meaning that the other party should walk away knowing exactly what to do.

Specific and actionable first means avoiding statements of generality like "you always" and "you never." Knowing that you've done something wrong a million times is neither useful nor actionable unless you own a time machine. Keep it specifically related to the conversation and future-focused. Frame your conversation in terms of real steps for improving in the future, versus a verbal beating regarding times that the other person was wrong.

Feedback should be aimed at improvement for the future that someone can actually complete. Because I'm obsessed with timeliness, a helpful example is, "I noticed that you showed up late for our meeting. It is important to honor everyone's time. Making others wait shows disrespect, which is not the right mind-set for beginning

Actionable vs. Rude

One example of rude rather than actionable feedback comes from famous entrepreneur Tyra Banks. Someone once told her she was too fat for a photo shoot, to which she said something along the lines of, "Thank you. There is absolutely nothing I can do to change that, so you've just made me feel like shit for no reason." I absolutely adore this example because telling someone to, say, lose 15 pounds for an upcoming modeling shoot is specific and actionable, whereas telling them they're currently unfit is just plain rude and useless.

a meeting. In the future, try to get here 10 minutes early so you don't accidentally appear disrespectful. And if you have a schedule change, send a quick text or e-mail so everyone gets an extra 10 minutes of their day." Notice how that removes personal fault from the situation.

DEPERSONALIZE FEEDBACK

Nobody likes feeling attacked. Nobody. Receiving statements in a threatening way about what you did or didn't do feels horrible. Reducing the resistance to feedback will amp up the likelihood of it being well received. Take out the personal stuff and replace it with statements of fact. "You didn't show up on time" doesn't work nearly as well as, "When someone is late, it appears disrespectful to others."

In personal matters, depersonalizing is actually more important, because couples have some magical superpower for holding on to negative or attacking statements. For example, "You're so rude for being late" will cause an argument that wastes at least an hour. Instead, "Next time, text me if you're running late" gets the point across, minus the drama.

Timing Is Everything

There's a study among behavioral psychologists that has been employed by pickup artists. The study shows that if you hesitate to say something for more than three seconds, you will almost never say it. Pickup artists say never hesitate: when you think you want to say hello to someone attractive, just do it. Set your intention and go.

Outside of bars, this language, intention, and action rule applies to most communications. If you want to, decide you will and do it. Wait until you're alone for the substantive conversation, of course. But saying, "Hey, let's chat offline" during or after the meeting is a good signal that you're meaning to carry through.

And do carry through as soon as you can. The closer in proximate time you are to the event, the more emotionally connected that person is to their work. For example, right after a presentation you are far more emotionally invested in receiving feedback than, say, a week after it.

As a general rule, I always say not to let things fester. When it comes to communicating, getting it done quickly leaves everyone feeling better soon after. Don't drag it out.

RECEIVING CRITICAL FEEDBACK

Unfortunately, not everyone is like you. Most people aren't studying how to be better communicators right now, and the people who aren't are the ones that probably need it the most. Mail them a copy of my book. (Just kidding!) If you run across such a person, the best way to prevent them from ruining your day is to adequately prepare yourself for some less-than-tactful, honest feedback.

This approach essentially reverse engineers the preceding skills for an empathetic and open mind-set that will allow you to learn, be your best, and avoid (or at least minimize) hurt feelings.

First, when you begin to feel angered or upset, pause for a second. Walk through the other person's intentions and alternative scenarios. Yes, okay, they were rude. But if their intentions were to help you, then maybe they're just a bad communicator. And if the alternative scenario could be to, say, fire you, then maybe this isn't all so bad.

It's hard to swallow the pill of criticism, but outside your own comfort zone is exactly the place that you will, in fact, grow as a person. Depersonalize the feedback by taking your personal emotions out of the picture and focusing on the specific and actionable steps you can take to improve yourself. Feel free to ask if it isn't clear. (More details on this to come.)

Open Up the Dialogue

Give your open, honest feedback, but then open up the room for discussion: "Do you disagree with me on this?" This is a great way to get people to buy in and own their areas for improvement. If they push back, there's no need for argument. Probe further into the conversation until you can reach a consensus. Honest feedback isn't received until it is owned by the recipient.

Depersonalize the Criticism

Becoming defensive over criticism is a natural human approach. But you are no natural, you're skilled. Restrict the burning desire to jump up and react. Or if you're the introverted type, don't immediately internalize. Stop for a moment, take a breath, and remember why this is happening. Unless the person actually hates you, they're most likely just trying to help. A poor execution doesn't mean bad intentions. Remind yourself that there is good intent here. Then, assess what the critic is trying to recommend. If it seems like it would help for you to take some new steps, by all means take them.

An ignorant person lets personal feelings stand in the way of potential. A wise one sees everything as an opportunity for growth. I'm all about a growth and learning mind-set as I find that it serves me, and most humans, far better than a closed or fixed mind-set. By that, I mean make it your goal to learn. Ignore the temptation of having hurt feelings.

You can best practice this skill by noticing when your feelings are hurt and using that as a cue to trigger yourself to laugh. Laughter eases the room and the soul. Then, take a moment to thoughtfully approach the conversation at hand. Ask open questions. If you need, state simply, "I would feel more open to understanding if this were less personal. Can we discuss this in a less personal way so that we can make it the most productive for both of us?" Even the biggest of dickheads can't refuse the opportunity to teach a lesson, so an approach like this is generally a good one.

Ask for Feedback That Is Specific and Actionable

Feeling annoyed by some random onslaught of criticism? Ask simply, "Can you give me action steps for the future?" If someone wants to help, they will. If someone wants to complain, they'll probably do that instead. In the latter case, I would recommend utilizing a hypnosis tool. Imagine that life is like watching a television show. Hear the volume of the speaker. Imagine you have a dial on the television. Turn the dial down—all the way down to zero.

At some later time, you can reanalyze the conversation for bits of usefulness or revisit the conversation when emotions have subsided. Heated conversations aren't the place for feedback, so just keep calm, carry on, and wait for a time when both parties can take a levelheaded approach. A lot of people call this being the bigger person, but I call it maintaining control of the situation. When someone decides that a conversation is heated, it is their choice—don't get baited.

Say Thank You and Request a Follow-Up

It is most often the case that you will receive criticism from a manager or other authority figure. Show them that you are taking things seriously. Say thank you and request a follow-up conversation in a few weeks or months to review progress. Integrity is important, and people who commit to growth and learning get extra brownie points for speaking their value.

"Sounds good. I will take this advice. Let's chat in two weeks to discuss our progress." Not *my* progress, *our* progress. This is a joint commitment. Giving someone a chance to see you overcome a weakness will solidify the kind of relationship that leaves them with a great taste in their mouth, versus the bad one they've got now. Every single communication you have is a chance to win. Ditto your personal relationship as well.

"You're right. I will take this seriously. Let's revisit in a few weeks to see if you're still unhappy." Boom, fight ended. Back to happy time. But I'm not joking—commit to action if you say it. Otherwise, don't commit to action. Lack of integrity is the root of poor communication. When words don't meet actions, you're finished.

As an aside, I've published this tip in the past as a way to speed your rate of getting promotions. It works as both an accountability hack and a means of speaking your value. Once you've improved the skill, you have before you an excellent opportunity to seek congratulations and raise your esteem. By communicating that you have successfully achieved a task, it speaks value to what you bring to the table in business. And the more you can vocalize that value, the greater your chances of getting a promotion or raise when you ask.

KEY CONCEPTS

- Start with why; remind the person that you care about them and want them to succeed
- Feedback is a two-way dialogue; ask open questions and reach consensus to the desired goal
- Make feedback specific and actionable
- Make feedback around statements of fact, not personal statements about the person
- Give feedback as soon after the event as possible
- When receiving feedback, ask for it to be specific and actionable
- When receiving feedback, try to analyze and depersonalize so you can receive the message and reduce the personal offense
- Say thank you and request a follow-up to review progress

ASK YOURSELF

Giving and receiving feedback can be a real pain in the ass. The essential steps to take for doing both is to ask yourself the following: "How do I depersonalize the feedback? How do I make it specific and actionable? How can I show, or personalize, that this is happening because we care about each other?" Finally, commit to learning. There's really no such thing as bad feedback so long as it is well intentioned. It's a critical way that we as humans can learn and grow from one another.

ASSERTIVENESS IS AN ART *AND* A SKILL

Raise your words, not your voice.
It is rain that grows flowers, not thunder.

—**RUMI**, POET

All political views aside, Barack Obama is considered one of the greats at public speaking—but he is also considered terrible in private settings. Democrats lost about 1,000 seats in Congress during his two terms as president. His lack of assertiveness in small settings is what many believe was at least partly responsible during midterm elections. He was kind of awkward and not so dynamic in smaller settings. The midterm election crowds weren't impressed. He still managed to win both terms in office, but the Republicans swung back in the midterms and split his Congress for the remainder of his presidency.

Public speaking and assertiveness are completely separate skills. Both must be learned and practiced. That will ensure that your leadership transcends large audiences. Holding a crowd is incredibly powerful, but at the end of the day, you've got to hold individuals' attention. Great communicators are trusted and believed at their word by individuals.

What is assertiveness, exactly? Assertiveness is the subtle art of leadership. You lead the dance, others follow. Assertiveness done wrong is called abrasiveness. The key difference lies in your audience: people don't want to be told what to do directly, but they do want an authoritative figure who minimizes available options and leads them to a good conclusion. See the difference?

Forbes published in 2013 that assertiveness is literally the key to good leadership. Leaders with good judgment but low assertiveness had a 4 percent chance of being ranked as effective. But with good judgment and high assertiveness, the number jumped to 71 percent.

STATEMENTS, NOT QUESTIONS

The most powerful technique I have ever learned in assertiveness came from studying pickup artists' techniques. Their goal is to make you more attractive, which means becoming more skillfully assertive. I use this trick in every business communication and in every text message. It's improved my response rate immeasurably. Pickup artists say that you must use statements. Questions make you appear weak and needy. Statements make you appear matter-of-fact. People like matter-of-fact.

For instance, "Will you go out to dinner with me tomorrow?" is unlikely to receive a yes. "I'm going to dinner tomorrow at 7 p.m. to Lobster Bar, please come" is more assertive, appealing, and far more likely to get the desired response. Don't give people a chance to say no. Communicate to the *yes*.

Minimize the Choices

An example I use with prospective clients: "Let's chat by phone this week. Send me what time you are available tomorrow." This is far more effective than, say, "Would you like to chat by phone this week?" This tool becomes far more important and effective during emotionally charged situations. By minimizing the amount of choices you give someone, you maximize the chances of getting to your intended outcome.

Practice by writing your sentence, and if a question mark belongs at the end of it, rephrase it as a statement. Inject assertiveness into every text and e-mail. Once this becomes routine, incorporate it into your speaking style, as well. "Let's go for a drink! See you at Lobster Bar at 7 p.m." Voila.

The Powerful Aphrodisiac of No

First, know your value. Then, speak your value. This will involve embracing the word *no*. If you can identify yourself as falling into the category of the proverbial "yes man", you may be thinking: *This is too risky. What if I stop saying yes all the time and people stop liking me? I could get fired.* Reality check: Have you noticed how everyone else around you isn't bending over backward to please? That's because most of us know that *yes* is what makes you a pushover, and speaking to your own values and boundaries is what earns you respect (even admiration). Take this tip from the most successful business people: learn the art of no.

Your Break-Even Point

If you're running your own business, there simply has to be a break-even point at which something is just not worth your time to take on. Everyone appreciates knowing this. How can you articulate your break-even point? Try this phrase: "Beyond this price, it simply doesn't cover our costs and our time."

This skill begins by understanding your own values and boundaries. Do a self-assessment. When do you feel violated or used by your friends, family, or coworkers? In a business setting, what is the determining factor at which a project simply isn't worth your time? Why is that?

Learn your own limits and write those down. The times you desire to be more assertive should be prepared for, as you're going to have to step outside your comfort zone a bit. When someone triggers your No button, say no firmly and state your why in a compelling way that makes it clear that this is simply an unreasonable idea, which no smart person would actually do. Turn no into your doing someone else a favor.

For example, there's a movement around mindfulness boundaries happening right now. New York and a few other states are even considering criminalizing after-hours e-mails. A great boundary you can set is the hours during which you are on and the hours during which you are off. It's easy to feel like your work must be 24-7. It makes you feel important, and it can drive you absolutely nuts. Shutting off completely during certain hours by setting those healthy boundaries and communicating the hours at which you will not be at work can raise your esteem with your colleagues. I did this with my Pilates class hours. At first, coworkers were not so thrilled at the frivolous boundary that from 7:30 a.m. to 8:30 a.m. I cannot be reached. But over time, they grew to respect and even value my personal time. You don't have to love Pilates, but you can set a good boundary around your dog or a hobby you love. So long as it is reasonable and doesn't interfere with your overall productivity, boundaries can be great for speaking your value. You're important and you deserve your time and space.

If you're working for someone else and you've been saying yes this whole time, chances are there are areas in your life that you will have to catch up in when it comes to asserting your personal boundaries. Do research and planning to prepare for these events. Every interaction is an opportunity to speak your value, so long as you know what that value is and aren't afraid to open your mouth.

Harvard Business Review recently reported a statistic that no job opportunity had ever been revoked by the applicant asking for more money. I say we apply this to every promotion, every love interest that seems out of our league, and every other damn thing we want and deserve in life. It doesn't hurt to say no and fight for a yes. Worst-case scenario: we end up in the exact same position we started in.

Plus, there is compelling psychology to the art of no. People want what they can't have, and when an option is made unavailable, the brain is naturally more curious for that option. It's called the information-gap theory. Use it to your advantage.

BALANCE ASSERTIVENESS WITH GOOD JUDGMENTS AND GOOD CHARACTER

There is a line that, once crossed, assertive techniques turn into, well, cocky steamroller techniques. While people do connect with assertiveness, it must be balanced with listening, honesty, connection, and making good judgments.

I once had an intern who had absolutely no experience, which didn't stop him from arguing with the extremely seasoned professionals on my team about things he knew nothing about. Don't be that guy or that woman. Making good judgments is the missing ingredient between assertiveness and abrasiveness.

Making good judgments requires a lot of preparation and some open ears. (Revisit chapter 1 for more on this.) Practice by asserting yourself carefully once you are confident in your knowledge or skills. Practicing assertiveness unwisely will lead you down a bad path at work and in your personal relationships.

Assume Good Intent

Another balancing factor for assertiveness is the mind-set for reaching mutual consensus over zero-sum games. Don't treat people like your enemies. Enemies can't be influenced. Approach situations as opportunities to reach mutual consensus. And don't be afraid to agree to disagree.

Assertive people aren't aiming to control situations; they are aiming to be heard in them. Be kind and show you care, and that will come off as authentic. Being aggressive or demanding isn't the way to seek friends. Assertive people don't need to make demands. Their actions speak for themselves.

Practice positive intent. Remind yourself before you engage in conversation that your goal is to lead, not conquer. Then approach with friendliness and maintain friendliness. Regardless of how heated other people may become, so long as you are true to yourself, your boundaries, and your positive intentions, the truth will shine through.

When to Assert Yourself

You should assert yourself whenever you want. When you want to lead, teach, and learn. When you feel uncomfortable and when you feel a boundary has been breached or a value has been compromised.

I can respect the fact that most people operate out of fear. You want that promotion, but you're afraid to be turned down. You want time with your friends but are afraid of disappointing your spouse, so you don't even bring it up. You want to take up a new activity, but you're afraid you may suck.

The Death Scenario

The next time you feel afraid, play through the objective scenarios in your head. If the most terrible scenario isn't death, then do it. Do exactly what you want. I welcome you to the winner's circle for living your best life.

Fear is a response meant to protect you from harm. Most of us are no longer out in the wild hunting animals for food, but that doesn't mean the fear gene has shut itself down. Fear exists in our head to prevent us from doing things—even things that will benefit us. That's where assertiveness can help. For example, research shows that assertiveness is key to overall relationship health because both partners are ensuring that their needs are met. Studies also show that people who learn assertiveness skills are happier and less stressed because their needs are increasingly met.

Here's the truth about fear: it's mostly a self-defeating fiction. This world was made for leaders. Stop listening to the fear bullshit and start leading. You'll gain more respect, more experience, and ultimately more freedom. Keep your response to it rational. But don't live in fear. Ever.

Assertiveness Is Good

People who live for others get passed over in life. People pleasers believe altruistically that they are doing right for themselves and for others, but when you truly describe the assertive person you realize that the person getting what they want is the one doing the best for themselves and others. Assertiveness is not a selfish approach. In fact, it's quite the opposite. Assertiveness is the art and skill of leading yourself and others to a better future together.

An example of this concept is Elon Musk. While everyone else was thinking about designing a nicer dash, he was designing a driverless system. When everyone else was thinking about paying the bills, he was creating interplanetary travel. I'm not suggesting you need grand ideas, but I do know that these things happened only because he asserted his radical ideas and people followed.

KEY CONCEPTS

- Speak with statements, not questions
- Remember that the word *no* is a powerful aphrodisiac
- Showing good judgment and good character is a key to assertiveness
- Assume good intent whenever you assert yourself by speaking to friends, not enemies
- Be assertive whenever and wherever you like; you'll feel happier and less stressed

ASK YOURSELF

During your next meeting, practice by checking on your words. Are you speaking in questions or statements? Aim for statements. Are you being too much of a yes-person? If so, assert a "no" in there. Set some boundaries. And when speaking, check in to be sure that you are operating from a place of authority. If not, it may not be the best time to assert yourself. Finally, check in to be sure you're operating from a place of positive intent. If the intent is bad or angry, take a step back. Assertiveness stems from a place of emotional control.

THE RHYTHM OF NEGOTIATION

Let us never negotiate out of fear.
But let us never fear to negotiate.

—JOHN F. KENNEDY

Everyone knows Jeff Bezos the billionaire. Few of us knew Jeff Bezos the book salesman. That's exactly where he started: selling books on the Internet. He stored them in his garage, packing orders and driving them to the post office himself. That was only 14 years ago at the time of this writing. Jeff had a plan and a big dream. He went to his friends, asking for investments to grow his business. The first people said no. The next few gave a small check of $5,000 or so. It took him more than 60 meetings, and only 20 people had said yes. The other 40 or so said no. Those 20 people who said yes had each given about $50,000 on average. Jeff had $1 million, and that was enough to build a business called Amazon.

Now, this sounds crazy. But what if a book salesman and acquaintance knocked on your door right now and asked you for a $50,000 check to grow his book business from his garage? Try to imagine if this happened to you in 1994? Bezos recalled that the first question people asked him was, "What is the Internet?"

Negotiation is the art of pushing forward through 40 people saying no to get to 20 others to say yes—learning what works, what doesn't, and how to sell people on a mutually beneficial alternate reality. You may not build Amazon or be able to explain what the Internet is to someone in 1994, but over time you'll increase positive responses, and that's a damn good start. It's all about practice.

NEGOTIATION IS A DANCE

Yoga is a flow state of meditation that all yogis aspire to. You move smoothly from one posture to the next. This flow state is the pattern of great negotiators. It's not a zero-sum game in which one party wins at the expense of the other. Negotiation is two or more parties dancing seamlessly together toward a future deal. Negotiations can create great partnerships from the beginning or a lot of hurt feelings that tarnish the relationship at the outset.

Negotiation will take more practice than the other skills in this book. It's often like great art: you know it when you see it, but defining it can be a bit tricky. In this chapter, we'll examine the foundations of great negotiation that, when practiced long enough, can have immeasurable influence on your communication skills. Any great negotiator will tell you that all communication is really negotiation. All leadership is negotiation. All we do is negotiate all day.

Let me explain. Human beings are often in a tug-of-war. There's what you want, what I want, and the consensus that happens somewhere between the two sides.

Do Your Research Beforehand

Learn as much as you can about the person you are negotiating with and what you will be negotiating about. If you're angling to get a raise, do your industry research on comparable salaries. If you want to sell a car, learn everything about the other cars people might be buying. Know your customer, know your product, and know the other available options. A good car salesperson can tell you specs. A great one can tell you why buying a BMW instead of their car is a terrible idea.

Based on Research

You should be able to say this in any negotiation: "Based on the research I have done, _____." For example, "Based on the research I have done, someone with my experience and background within my field is making 10 percent more than my proposed raise, across every single comparable industry." It is also vital that you should be prepared for probing and be able to answer further questions.

SET YOUR WALK POINT

Speaking of coming prepared, every great negotiator I know says that strong negotiators are always prepared to walk away. Define that precise point at which something is absolutely not worth your time, and prepare yourself to be able and ready to leave at that point. If that means creating a plan B, then do so.

What you need is a reason to not be so invested that you can't say no. When you can't say no, it's not a negotiation, it's just a struggle to get what you need at any price possible. That's no negotiation.

Find Out What the Other Person Wants or Needs

You're going to need to work with the person or people, not against them, which means understanding what mutually beneficial goal you're going to accomplish together. Revisit chapter 3 to figure this one out.

Everyone wants, seeks, or craves certain things. For some it's money, for others it's prestige. Often, people want to avoid pain or suffering. Empathize with the person's position beforehand to understand their goals. Then, your job is to paint yourself into their goals. The negotiation itself will be a mutual conversation about this very topic.

If you can prepare beforehand, great. If you can't, then it will take a lot of skill and practice to be able to figure out what people want on the fly. Ask open questions and listen fully to the person you are negotiating with. Using empathy, paint a powerful vision of the future in which both of you get your needs, wants, or goals met. This is going to be the primary focus of your conversation.

BUILD RAPPORT

It's crucial not to just walk up to people and bluntly ask for what you want from them. For the most part, people don't like that. Warm up your guest by building a rapport with them: find and discuss common interests, listen to their random ideas. Don't rush or get frustrated. Remember, this is a dance. Go with the flow.

The closer you are and the more you feel that you have in common, the better the flow. Find a good flow state with no friction before you launch into a negotiation. This can take minutes, hours, or months. It's all about that flow. You'll know that you are *in* flow when the conversation feels natural, the two of you feel close enough that you are comfortable discussing your prepared negotiation, and the context or environment won't interfere.

Context and Environment

Contextual interference is a real flow killer. For example, you're having a great conversation and the waiter comes in to interrupt. Or you're about to make a major point, but the meeting runs out of time. These are pure "damn it" moments. You should do your best to predict them and avoid them at all costs.

For instance, don't talk seriously until the food arrives. Check the clock to be sure you have active time left. Dive deep only when everyone's phone is down. This is precisely why some people love doing business over golf—there is little distraction, including the boring sport itself.

Think through the interaction as far in advance as you can. Practice the interaction in your head for those big flow moments. That's a long stretch of distraction-free runway space that you can use to your advantage. That's your strike point. You'll want to build rapport and then jump in at that right, distraction-free time.

YOU'RE FLEXIBLE, NOT FIXED

Fixed mind-set types ineffectively argue for positions. It's their way or it's the highway. Open mind-set types, on the other hand, are far more likely to get their way because there isn't one right answer, but a set of mutually beneficial options. And the truth is, there isn't just one right answer.

Rational choice theory was discovered by my friend and colleague Howard Moskowitz way back in the 1970s. He founded a behavioral economics principle by studying people's preferences at the grocery store. He discovered that there was no universally accepted right choice for the best-tasting product. Instead, there is a subset of correct choices that apply to different subsets of people. Thus, chunky spaghetti sauce was born. And extra-garlicky spaghetti sauce. And Diet Coke®. And Coke® Zero Sugar. His point was that if you try to create one perfect answer to please everybody, you're not going to please anybody. Instead of aiming for perfection, create a series of choices that, as a whole, capture your audience.

A good negotiator knows this. Take your absolute right answer and come up with a set of other available options that also work well for both of you. (For more on Howard's work, read his book, *Selling Blue Elephants*.)

Build a Pattern of Yes

When people agree with others, they will tend to agree with them again, through a kind of brain compliance we have built in. This brain compliance makes us want to act with consistency, so if we tend to agree with someone, then we will tend to agree with them again and again. You can use this to your advantage in any negotiation with a bit of advanced planning. As a precursor to the negotiation, allow for your listener to say yes.

Great examples of this are stopping to pause every so often to say, "Does that make sense?" Not in a pedantic way, but with a voice of genuine concern that you are keeping everyone on the same track.

These micro-commitments to a yes from your listeners will create a compliance factor in their heads that you can build on with more yeses.

Be sure to plan questions that seek yes as an answer and that preferably validate or somehow enhance the esteem of your audience. "Does that make sense?" *Yes, of course it does—I'm smart.* Or, "You know what I mean?" *Yes, of course I do—I'm smart.* Set up a trail of positive replies to increase your chances when you need one.

Who Calls the First Offer?

Knowing who calls the first offer is unclear because it's based on *your* psychology. Here is what I do know: the person who goes second and immediately accepts is much happier, but statistically they got the poorest deal. In other words, if you're really uncomfortable negotiating, this will not go well for you at all. If you are an overly aggressive type who has done very little research, your first offer could shut down the transaction entirely.

My best advice is to prepare well, aim higher than you intend, and if you get inquisitive faces, then justify the reasoning. Don't be afraid to push with reasoning and value, but don't get stuck on microscopic amounts. Ask first, aim high, and add a bit at the end.

Have a Set of Next Steps

People are far more likely to commit in the moment than they are even hours after a negotiation concludes. This means part of your planning is to have your next steps in hand and ready to go. Have your card reader ready to take a credit card, your contract ready to sign (even if you write the number in by hand and initial it, that still counts)—but be ready to *really* close.

The biggest rookie mistake by salespeople is believing that the deal closes at verbal agreement. There should always be a contract or cash exchange, or you never made a deal at all. Anyone who has ever had a week pass or a client flake knows exactly how these cop-outs feel.

KEY CONCEPTS

- Build rapport until you hit a flow state
- Come well researched and prepared
- Set a walk point at which you are able and willing to say no
- Tap into an unmet want or need in the other person
- Plan for a good context and environment in which you won't get disrupted
- Have a series of mutually beneficial resolutions available to you
- Build a pattern of yes
- Offer your very best first
- Ask for a little more at the end
- Have a tangible set of next steps to solidify the deal

ASK YOURSELF

Before your next negotiation, ask yourself: "Am I prepared in an understanding of the market, competitors, and my product or service? What is my set point at which I'm willing to walk away? What does this person really want or need? How can I meet that? Where is a place in the flow of this conversation that I won't be interrupted, so I can dive into the hard sell? How can I get this person (or people) to respond with small yeses and commitments? What is my researched high offer that I will call first? And finally, what are the next steps once the deal is closed, and how can I have them right in front of me when needed?"

9

BECOME A MASTER OF CONFLICT

For good ideas and true innovation, you need human interaction, conflict, argument, debate.

—**MARGARET HEFFERNAN,** EXECUTIVE, AUTHOR, AND TED SPEAKER

I can't think about the word *conflict* without the face of Steve Jobs appearing in my head. Former employees at Apple and NeXT often tell stories about his unreasonable demands and his absolute refusal to accept facts that didn't fit what he wanted to believe. And yet, we love him. He pushed people to create things they didn't believe were possible. It would be easy to pretend that if Steve Jobs were still alive today, you or I would want to work for him. He's become a legend but the truth is, working for him would probably be pretty bad. But I think I would anyway. Would you?

Let's contrast that with the modern workplace with its politics, niceties, and seeking of consensus. Yes, it's important that everyone gets along on some level. But I wish there was a place somewhere between Steve Jobs shouting at me in an office and a smiling, happy workplace. I think conflict is overlooked and underutilized in business, mostly because people are doing it all wrong. It doesn't have to be scary stuff; in fact, if you reframe conflict, it can create greatness.

I particularly love conflict, because I love things like innovation and diversity. Think about it: if you're all sitting in a room nodding your heads at each other in agreement, you may want to go find a different room. If your goal is to embrace learning and growth, then you need to become comfortable and even master alternative ways of thinking and embracing differing perspectives.

BE OPEN TO CONFLICT

As hard as this may sound, recognize that moments of conflict are opportunities for deeper connection and communication in the future. How you approach conflict sets the tone for any relationship. It's far harder to change a standard down the road than it is to create one from the beginning.

Conflict is an opportunity to reach a better level of understanding. If you are open to the first instance, it's more likely that future instances will be less stressful, as you've set the tone for openness. On the other hand, if you shut down from conflict, you've also set a standard: that you will be a difficult person to deal with in the future. In business culture, this can create a fear of communication. People simply won't want to be open and express themselves to you, meaning things get missed and real leadership becomes harder and harder. This also applies to personal relationships.

When conflict comes at you, it is pretty easy to spot from an emotional sense. Someone is having a hard time approaching you with a conversation, and they may be heated, scared, or even upset. Your first job is to expressly communicate your openness. Use phrases like "Let's talk", or "We can talk about anything—tell me what's going on." Assertive statements that acknowledge and accept whatever may come will set the right tone for the present and the future.

If you are faced with the position of a long-term relationship that hasn't been open in the past, there's nothing wrong with acknowledging that in order to reset the expectation: "I recognize that we've had a hard time speaking in the past, so let's change that now." The first conflict chat may get a bit icky, but if you're in it for the long term, it will be worth it.

Discussion > Statements

I once watched a powerful CEO reset a conflict situation with extreme authority and ease. His words completely changed the energy of the room. A series of e-mails had been sent back and forth, escalating an issue. Both sides had their position, and neither side was particularly correct. It would have been easy to host the meeting, pretending like all of that hadn't happened and letting both sides sit and secretly hate each other. That's the problem with e-mails. Statements and assertions are easy, but discussion that solves a problem can be tricky when it's just one side sending the e-mail and cc'ing the other.

This CEO walked in the room, acknowledged the conflict, and reset the tone entirely. "Listen, I know a series of e-mails has gone back and forth and escalated a situation. I want us to all change that now. On my side, I understand that my team is open to working together to constructively improve our standing through this collaboration, and if yours is as well, then we should all agree to put this behind us and align our interests to making that happen."

"I Just Want Us to Be Good."

My publicist may be the greatest master of conflict I've ever met. She's in communications for a living, which helps, sure. But when a situation arises, she goes out of her way to dive right in. She expresses all of the reasons she cares about the person and all of the things she likes about them, and then says, "I just want us to be good. What can we do to make that happen?" It works every time.

No one could argue. If you argued, you were not aligned to the right things. That's the great thing about alignment and framing. Which brings me to the next section.

Seek Ways to Align Your Common Interests

Researchers at UC Berkeley did a study of couples and conflict and found that conflict can actually help deepen a relationship when the couples believed that they understood each other. Conflict, therefore, is all in the perception. If you believe someone doesn't understand you, conflict can damage you. But if you feel understood, conflict can bring you closer. The point here is simple: seek ways to understand each other and conflict can be of benefit.

Purely arguing from *your* position is never going to work. Speak to what you can both agree on. Reframe the conversation as progress to working toward that goal. This can be as simple as stating, "Let's work toward understanding each other better so that this conflict doesn't happen again, or at least happens less frequently."

In most instances, people don't want to be in conflict. On the other hand, some people enjoy it. If you run into a person who seeks out conflict, then understand that they love to be heard and they love intense situations that achieve a result. When that's the case, the aligned interests can easily be around just that. "Let's avoid all the conflict and work toward achieving a result we both want to have. What is it that you need, and how can we get there together?" Aligning to a common goal takes you from opposition to being two people on the same team.

TAKE AWAY THE TECHNOLOGY

Dale Carnegie wrote one of the greatest books of all time on resolving conflict: *How to Win Friends and Influence People.* Unfortunately, he wasn't alive to witness our digital communications revolution. As hard as this may seem, when you approach a space where conflict is or may occur, you absolutely have to communicate in the real world. UCLA researchers have found that the words in an e-mail or text alone account for only 7 percent of the information in a communication, which explains why your e-mail joke didn't go so well that time, and also why so many conflicts arise from e-mail.

Pick up your phone, open your video messenger, or head to the person directly, if you can. That other 93 percent of communication you're going to need to resolve the conflict is 55 percent facial expressions and body language and 38 percent voice and tone. Without all that, the communication is going nowhere. Empathy does lead to efficiency. E-mails and texts lead to miscommunication. Pick up your phone.

DON'T FALL VICTIM TO CONTROL AND BULLYING TACTICS

Some people don't fight fair and may seek to control or intimidate you during a conflict. We've all seen this happen before: yelling, piling on insults, escalating, ignoring.

These are all ways that others try to control and bully you during a conflict. The person isn't trying to resolve the conflict at all, they're just aiming to control you and the situation. When you spot one of these tactics, you'll need your own counterbalance to keep yourself in control so that you aren't victimized by a pressured situation. It's all about learning the right skills in advance to maintain control over yourself so that conflict can be *mutually* resolved.

The Three Common Bullying Tactics

Shouting, or even threatening to shout at someone, is the most basic of the bullying tactics during a conflict. If and when this ever happens, you will not control the situation by shouting back. You will control the situation by simply pausing the conversation so that emotions can de-escalate. Some people choose to leave the room. I prefer a short pause and a little manipulation tactic I'll teach you here. The secret lies in psychology. No one wants to appear or be called emotionally out of control. By simply calling someone emotional, an ego gets offended. With this in mind, my favorite de-escalation technique is to say, "We should continue this conversation at a later time when you are emotionally in control," or, "Please control your emotions." That, in itself, is pretty inflammatory, so you'll need to practice delivering it in a caring and non-condescending way. By simply pointing out that someone is emotionally out of control, you've just left them with no option but to get in control. Don't be surprised if someone shouts back in response, "I am in emotional control!" At this point I often laugh, agree, and pause with a caring face until the person simply calms down. With a little practice, you can train yourself and others around you that shouting isn't going to fly so long as you are around.

The second bullying tactic is the opposite of shouting: someone refuses to communicate at all and completely ignores you. This is another control tactic meant to own the conversation and victimize you in the process. Much like being called emotional, people really don't like to be told they're acting immaturely. A similar process works here. Simply state, "I see that you are ignoring me. Is there a more mature approach we could take here?" Again, it takes practice to master these lines. Come from a place of authenticity and caring to resolve the conflict. Acknowledge the bullying tactic and seek a friendly alternative. Don't be controlled by it.

The third bullying tactic is to speak in inflammatory statements. One common example is saying something like, "Fine, I'll do it all myself!" Same approach here. Pause and say, "That is one approach—is there a less extreme alternative we could take?" Using reference and framing language like *less extreme* or *more productive* is a way to nudge people back into a more reasonable mind-set.

Nobody wants to act like an idiot—some people just can't help themselves. Counterbalance bullying tactics with a little friendly name-calling of your own. By framing it as calm and caring ways of bringing the communication back into a reasonable place, you can keep everything in a controlled state where productive communication can actually occur.

APPROACH ALL CONFLICT AS A LEARNING OPPORTUNITY

As I mentioned in the beginning of this chapter, I love conflict. It can be a source for learning and growth if you utilize it and approach it correctly. In my mind, a conflict is simply a place where two people believe different things, and there is some universal truth out there, somewhere between them.

The incorrect approach to conflict is what leads most of us down the wrong path. For instance, if you are listening to someone who is saying something completely ignorant, it's pretty normal to want to jump in and correct: "Well, actually, no, Bigfoot is not real, and the sky is not made of angel particles, and you're an idiot."

How you respond is the difference between conflict and continuous learning. The preceding example is a great lesson in what not to do. Telling people that they are flatly wrong or name-calling will only lead to an insulted audience and no one will be any better off.

Your Intentions During a Conflict

Let's start with the right intentions. Your goal for conflict should always be to better yourself and better others, so that you can both benefit from the transaction. This means not focusing on your truth or their truth, but *the* truth. I think it's easy to get stuck in one's own version of truth. If that's the case, don't bother. Don't be willing to debate unless you're willing to learn. Approach all conflicts from an open mind-set that no one is right or wrong and both of you are seeking the truth or right answer.

What won't work at all is simply calling someone wrong. That brings you into opposing positions. You want to stay aligned toward the truth together. When done correctly, challenges breed solutions. Conflict breeds innovation. When ideas converge, great things happen. How those ideas converge is up to you. An enlightened leader will recognize and lean into conflicting situations in a way that makes everyone better for it. This means taking on challenges, yes, but from a place of mutual respect.

When you are inspired to start a conflict, remember Dale Carnegie's statement: "Nine times out of ten, an argument ends with each of the contestants more firmly convinced than ever that he is absolutely right." A conflict won't feel like a conflict at all once you master these skills.

Depersonalizing Statements & Questions

When the right mind-set is there, jump into challenges with two skills: (1) making depersonalizing statements and (2) asking questions. Making depersonalizing statements means taking the positions away from the other person completely. Instead of "You said _____," keep it to the facts and statements only. No discussion of people, just the topic at hand. For example, you can say, "I understand that <statement>, but have you considered <alternative fact>?"

And that brings us to the second skill: asking questions. This is about leading someone down the path to an alternative truth. If someone says something you don't agree with, ask a question. For example, "What are your thoughts on <the alternative>?" or, "Have you considered _____?" The space between you and the other person will lead you both somewhere better. And this means you're going to be leading with questions.

KEY CONCEPTS

- Approach conflict as an opportunity for deeper connection and understanding
- The more in-person the better; never use e-mail or text (video and phone are okay)
- Align your interests so you're both working through a conflict on the same team
- Spot, point out, and minimize bullying tactics like yelling, ignoring, or inflammatory statements to avoid getting hijacked by a conflict
- Handle conflict with depersonalizing statements and questions to get to the truth

ASK YOURSELF

The next time you're faced with a potential or actual conflict, check in with yourself and ask: "How can I use this to deepen our connection?" If you notice a conflict arising, ask: "How can I drop this communication vehicle and take us as in-person as possible?" Phone, digital communication, or face-to-face encounters are the best methods. During the discussion, ask: "How can I make this so we both win in the resolution?" Also, spot and avoid bullying tactics with the following: "Is this person escalating? Ignoring me? Shouting? Hijacking the conversation?" By keeping a cool head and answering these questions, you can avoid the conflict going awry. Finally, always ask yourself: "Am I tied to my position, and if so, how can I let this go and be open to other opinions? How can I depersonalize this conversation from my version of the truth, and be open to alternative truths?" It never hurts to try. You might even learn something.

10

HOW TO DEAL WHEN THE STAKES ARE HIGH

If your dreams don't scare you, they are too small.

—**RICHARD BRANSON,** INVESTOR, ENTREPRENEUR, AND PHILANTHROPIST

otivational speaker Tony Robbins will talk for eight hours on the stage in a given day. We think of him as a strong and powerful figure now, but when I met him, he reminded me of a very simple fact: that he helped push motivational speaking seminars into the mainstream. Tony described the struggle of booking speaking engagements early in his career, of not being taken seriously because motivational speaking seemed soft and fluffy, and of rejection after rejection after rejection in his early career. He even described that once he was nearly arrested for an event. He was hosting a seminar in Vancouver and the Canadian government intervened, stating that he did not have a work visa to perform in the country and that if he tried to host his seminar, he would be arrested. Faced with disappointing fans or a visit to Canadian jail, most of us would have given up. But Tony described in detail the plan he hatched, which involved renting buses, moving all of his participants across the border (where he then hosted his seminar on US soil), and taking them back to Canada at the end of the day.

PREPARING WHEN THE STAKES ARE HIGH

In many ways, everything you have read in this book has prepared you for this chapter. Struggle and perseverance when the stakes are high is where great leadership is made. High-stakes communication is your ability to think on your feet, persevere, be creative, and manage through fear, stress, loss, and situations that may feel impossible.

Whether you are sitting in a courtroom or in the human resources department, this chapter is about how to operate out of high levels of fear. Fear is powerful. Fear of loss, whether it's financial or emotional, is a much stronger motivator for people than our desire for gain. In fact, the most powerful marketing agencies on earth work through our basic human fear of rejection. Our desire to fit in drives the fashion industry, the cosmetics industry, and the cosmetic medical industry, among many others. We're terrified of social rejection. We're terrified of financial loss. That's all normal, but what do you do when it comes to communicating in such a situation?

High-stakes communication occurs at any moment where we feel physically or emotionally out of control. Some people are amplified under stress, and others shut down from it. Regardless of your emotional response, there are skills to be learned. Running a successful business, health care practice, or household requires that we deal with high-stress environments. The most important factor is that you manage communication with others within these stressful contexts. Because it's when everything breaks down that communication really matters. That's what separates the superheroes from the rest of us. It's a split-second reaction. The best plan ahead, look for these moments, and take advantage of them. High-stakes communication is a skill set that can be developed and practiced so that when you land flatly into such a position, you're able to handle it like a pro.

The Dwyane Wade Mind-Set

Before we jump into the communication skills you need, let's start with getting your mind-set in the right place. This is the most common coaching technique I use when mentoring leaders across the country. I'm a huge Miami Heat fan, so I use Dwyane Wade for this thought experiment, but choose any professional athlete you like.

When you're preparing for a high-stakes event, it's easy to become your own worst enemy. In fact, your brain by default works this very way. You start playing through the worst possible scenarios: "What if I fall? What if I forget my lines? What if everyone hates my presentation and I get fired, then have to go home and explain to my family?" This is common, yes. But it's sure not productive.

When I mentor leaders, if I catch someone playing the negative mind-set game with themselves, I simply ask: "What do you think Dwyane Wade is thinking when he walks out onto the basketball court? Do you think Dwyane Wade isn't thinking, *What if I fall or what if I miss*?" It sounds silly to even state that out loud. Letting your fear get the best of you and running through all sorts of negative scenarios is equally silly. Professional athletes are trained in how to build a winning mind-set because it is crucial to their performance outcomes.

The Winner's Mind-Set

Here, I will break down the basics for you into a short exercise that you absolutely must do before any high-stakes communication. Athletes begin by getting pumped up to a favorite song. Whether it's "Eye of the Tiger" or another song you love, get your headphones on and turn the volume up. (I should note that Tony Robbins follows this process before every public appearance, as do most other celebrities and performers you see on television.)

Step two is to build your mental state up to feeling really confident, motivated, and determined. Work yourself up to that motivated state and visualize yourself winning your desired goal. Visuals are extremely important here. Visualize your feelings after you've just achieved your goal. Lock that visual association into your mind and hold on to it. Now you're in the winner's mind-set.

If you feel yourself slipping out of that visualization and those feelings, play your song to cue those reminders all over again, as often as you need. The key is to stay focused on a powerful visual of your future and avoid any negative thoughts that may hinder your goal.

Mind-set will inform everything you do. Confidence is one of the key factors to successful communication in high-stakes situations. This is your shortcut to your most confident mind-set ever. Use it often.

CREDIBILITY

Credibility is a determining factor for whether people will trust you and be influenced by you. Your ability to think on your feet and respond instantaneously in the moment is critical, and it happens long before the communication. Think through any possible question that could come from your audience and do your research. You don't have to have the answer to everything, but you should at least be able to point to references and give your audience access to more information.

We're essentially describing the profession of a lawyer here. Lawyers prepare research for weeks just to walk into a courtroom and have a discussion that generally lasts under one hour. The most well-researched and credible argument is the winning one. Treat every high-stakes communication this way. Don't shy away from bringing a reference list to your high-stakes event. Research shows your credibility and builds the level of trust you require from your audience to win the day.

AUTHENTICALLY CARE

If you've prepared well, people will see that you are a credible source. The next part is to capture their attention and create influence. A lot of people make the rookie error of believing that they need to act very confident in a high-stakes situation. As if acting confident can mask your secret fears and anxieties. This is simply untrue. When people try to act overconfident to mask their fears, that's when they land in the obnoxious-personality zone, which is a big turnoff.

The key to delivering when the stakes are high is to instead embrace your authenticity. Not all of it, but utilize certain parts. I want to be very clear about this point, because many people hear the word *authenticity* and assume it means *just be yourself. Just*

Meeting a Superhero

In the aftermath of the 2012 shooting that occurred in an Aurora, Colorado, movie theater, my friend Dan Oates, who was the Aurora chief of police at the time, became a national news figure. I remember watching him talk and break down in tears. Whatever was going through his mind at the time was not going to be masked. The situation was awful and his authenticity in that moment forever solidified him as a leader in my mind. I met him much later when he became chief of police in my city, and I remember feeling like I was actually meeting a superhero.

My point is that leaning into your emotional side during high-stakes situations will not make you look weak. It will make you appear real. People value real caring. As the maxim goes, "Nobody cares about how much you know, until they know how much you care."

be yourself is actually terrible advice in most situations, especially in high-stakes situations, because if you're really just being yourself, you would walk in and say, "Hi, I really need this job so I can pay my rent," or some other sort of honesty that wouldn't serve you well when you're trying to get something you want or need.

Instead, I'm referring to your ability to tap into the authentic care that you feel for the situation. Passion cannot be faked. Displaying authentic care has been shown to improve patient satisfaction scores in hospitals, heighten customer satisfaction, and create customer loyalty even when things go really, really wrong.

Authentically show that you care about the situation. You can do this by tapping into your why. Why is this so important to you? Why is this so important for the other person? What are those reasons that you care and that they should care?

When you set this up in your mind, it manifests to the world in your words and actions. If you get stuck along the way, reach back into that why statement—purpose-driven communication may not always be objectively perfect, but it will hook the audience into understanding you and believing in you. And that's the key for influence in tough situations.

GRIT

Grit is both a communication skill and a mind-set. Psychologist Angela Duckworth and many others have spent years and years researching what makes some people succeed while others fail. They found that it was not aptitude, personality, or socioeconomic status. There was no single factor that accounted for success versus failure except one: grit.

Grit is defined as the perseverance of your effort and the consistency of your effort. From a skills-building perspective, this means that having grit assures that you will absolutely continue forward and not give up, even in the face of near failure.

You will do this because you will remember that it is your key to success. Whether students won or lost competitions came down to grit. Whether salespeople succeeded or failed in their careers came down to grit. Hundreds of studies have been conducted on the topic, and grit is what wins the day.

When you feel like you're going to fail, keep going. When you think you can't, keep going.

Step-by-Step

For an in-depth study of behavioral change, I highly recommend you read BJ Fogg's work. He's the mastermind behind the Stanford Behavior Design Lab. I was lucky enough to be accepted into one of his boot camps at Stanford and it changed my view of life.

BJ says that by making something simpler to do and breaking it down into steps, you are more able to do it and therefore more likely to do it. So, let's apply this to communication. If you're giving a talk to an audience and get a case of the nerves, just keep going to the next slide. Just that next slide. If you're in a negotiation room and your career depends on the deal, don't think about the magnitude of the deal, just think about your next bullet point. If you feel like you may give up exercise altogether, drop it to eight reps instead of ten. The net result of all this work is the perseverance of effort and consistency of effort that creates your inner grit in any situation.

A useful trick for helping you achieve an attitude of grit comes from the world of personal training. If you've ever had a personal-training session, you know that it's the personal trainer's job to push you beyond your limits in physical fitness through a repetition of movements. You will eventually hit that point where you cannot go any further and you want to give up. "Ten more!" the trainer shouts at you. You just don't have ten in you and can't lift your arms at all. But then, your trainer uses a mental trick and says, "Okay, give me eight."

Suddenly, you are able to move your arms again. And the magic part here is that it was only a two-rep difference. Your trainer got you to add eight more reps immediately. This is because when you break something down into smaller, easier steps, it motivates your brain to act. When the task at hand gets simpler, you believe you are more able to do that task, you become more motivated to do that task, and you are far more likely to do that task.

KEY CONCEPTS

- Confidence is vital; develop the winner's mind-set
- Credibility requires research; prepare yourself for every scenario
- Be authentic in your purpose and convey true emotional care
- Consistently persevere through struggles and failures by breaking projects down into simple steps, and keep going

ASK YOURSELF

When the stakes are high, first ask yourself: "What would Dwyane Wade do?" Then, "How can I show my credibility? How can I show I genuinely care?" And finally, if you fail, ask yourself: "Am I going to let myself become a failure, or am I able to keep going?" Then keep going.

11
Bonus

HOW TO AVOID A #METOO SITUATION

*I want to thank everyone who broke their silence
this year. . . . We see you, we hear you,
and we will tell your stories.*

—**REESE WITHERSPOON,** ACTOR AND PRODUCER

A powerful female executive sat in a meeting with a potential client. The prospect and her male COO chatted at length, then went out for drinks after. The chatting and drinking continued, and she eventually called it a night to leave them to it. The next day she called the prospect: "There is a reason that my business card says CEO," she explained. "What my colleague and I are aware of and want you to know is that you barely made eye contact with me or included me in your conversation throughout the entire day. I want you to know this."

She never heard from the prospective client again.

Stories of gender-based misconduct are bubbling up and the role that men and women have with each other when it comes to work is dramatically shifting. The #MeToo movement, begun in 2006 by community organizer Tarana Burke, has now sparked a social conversation that we cannot ignore.

It would be easy to say, "Well, I haven't rubbed my genitals on anyone, so I'm not part of the problem." Easy to say, yes, but untrue. #MeToo may have gone viral in 2017 with overt high-profile callouts of physical assault of women by men in positions of power, but it has uncovered a cultural dynamic that we've all known has existed since women began working. The waters have muddied, and this chapter is designed to keep you protected when it comes to interpersonal work relationships.

EXPAND OUR UNDERSTANDING OF MISCONDUCT BASED ON SEX

Step one is to expand the concept of sexual misconduct to conduct that is sexual, nonconsenting, and typically based on sex or gender identity and power dynamics. So, with this expanded definition, we can take steps to solve for this. Remember that it's not about any overt action but in the million little pieces of interactions between humans. We're not just talking the sexually explicit stuff here. There are ways that we all could sacrifice a bit of control and become more inclusive to each other. The truth is a lot of this stuff is based on dominance, which means you will have to sacrifice a bit of control. Be a bit more open.

I believe most of us don't actively wish to have segregation, sexism, misogyny, or harassment in our lives. What we suffer from is a lack of awareness for ways we're causing more harm than good for each other. *The hidden ways.* Yes, there are predators out there. But what is more predatory than anything to women, minorities, and other exploited groups of people (including people of color and people on the LGBTQ+ spectrum) is power imbalance. We create and are comforted in power imbalances because they were always comfortable.

The prospective client in my true story at the beginning of this chapter may have just felt insecure next to a powerful and very beautiful female executive. He may have wanted to give her the impression that he was not sexually interested and decided it best to minimize eye contact and avoid a sexual advance. However, let's say this person came up in a corporate environment that does not value women or place them in powerful positions. He may have perceived her actions erroneously as scolding. Does this mean that the CEO was wrong in stating the obvious to her potential client? No, not at all. But his lack of response was incorrigible. I get that, and so should you.

Now, there's no way to overcome this national dilemma in a single book and definitely not in a single chapter. If you go out and write your children's movie about a powerful princess on Wall Street earning her credentialed respect, thank you. For the rest of us, what we can do is better understand each other and progress. With a little self-examination and by shifting our cultural norms and behaviors, we can resolve and avoid these possible issues for ourselves and others.

There is a great training on inclusion that was implemented in a technology organization I work with. It was very effective in creating more diversity and inclusion at work. Study after study about the lack of women in certain types of jobs kept finding that it wasn't that women weren't skilled for the jobs available. In fact, women very much wanted the jobs. It was the cultural norms in the organization that were creating barriers. Following are a few highlights that will help us all learn from the best and break down some barriers of our own.

UNDERSTAND THAT THIS CHAPTER IS FOR EVERYONE

The ugly reality is that women harass each other all the time. The competitive social norms that exist between women in social life don't just magically disappear in the workplace. I recently read an article in *Inc.* that suggested that men and women shouldn't be mentors, for fear that it will incite jealousy and rumors by other women in the office. My argument is simply this: it is not a marginalized person's gender's duty to promote a harassment-free workplace. It is a leader's duty. Just because relatively fewer women are leaders today does not mean men can avoid this responsibility. This is why all leaders should make a promise: we will not harass each other, no matter what.

From here forward, there are no more excuses. Gender segregation at work is not a business solution. It's utter bullshit. Instead, let's all agree to a moral code of ethics for us well-intentioned people

Woman Interrupted

There's an app called Woman Interrupted that detects and counts how many times a woman is interrupted during a meeting. Download it to your phone as a subtle tactic for pointing out the obvious disparities. Plus, it's pretty funny.

to follow. I believe we can vision it and reinforce it with communication.

But first, we aren't truly seeing the magnitude of this problem. A study by McKinsey & Company found that in workplaces where 10 percent of leaders were women, 50 percent of men believed that women were well represented. "Just a few token women, in other words, makes it seem like the problem is solved," writes Emily Peck in response to these statistics. A few women leaders alone won't solve an endemic problem. What will solve the problem is for us, individually and collectively, to envision, lead, model, and reinforce the advancements in culture we would like to create. Language just happens to be a powerful tool for doing so.

Speaking of language, at this very moment women are getting talked over in meetings, receiving harsher performance reviews, and are about 70 percent less likely to get promoted, according to *USA TODAY*. Sounds kind of shitty? It is. Gentlefolk, tell your friends. Here are some communication skills we all need.

Talk About Inclusion to Create Inclusion

This seems pretty basic, but the first step to inclusion is talking about it. I wrote an article for *Entrepreneur* that states how leaders can build inclusion: "Stop writing more and more policies, and start paying attention to people. People want to be part of the group, and will follow social norms at great cost. Leaders must decide, and then follow through. Make gender equity a part of your daily conversation; empower people to hold equity accountable. Make it a fundamental. Lead with equity. Be sure it's not only stated, but that it filters through meetings and informal interactions."

Whether you're in a formal leadership role or not, simply open up dialogue. Ask your colleagues how they would like to communicate. Ask them if there are things that can improve. And if you notice someone being cut off or spoken over in conversation, please talk about it. For instance, women have such an unfair power imbalance that most of us are afraid to communicate about it at all.

While doing research for that *Entrepreneur* article, I found out that 75 percent of workplace harassment whistleblowers are retaliated against. The social norm is simply to shut your mouth if you want to keep your job. What you can do is work to change that. Let's all be badass, unafraid communicators, and say, "Hey, are we treating each other with absolutely awesome inclusion and what can we do better?"

Ban Gender-Normative Communication

Saying "Hi, sweetie" to a colleague may be well intentioned, but what it communicates to the recipient is, "I am a figure of dominance who has decided that you are a piece of drugstore candy." Drop the gender-normative dialogue altogether. It subversively displays your dominance and that just isn't very inclusive. Your goal is to create a level playing field for all. Ethnic, gender-based, and ableist slang needs to disappear completely. People are human. Pay close attention to the normative language you use.

There are gender-normative biases present in our language and very often in the media. You can practice and build your language-neutrality skills through careful self-examination. When you're interacting with someone with a different gender or sexual identity than you, stop and do a little self-audit on occasion: "Would I say that to a person who shares my identity?"

Women often get called things like "abrasive" and "difficult". If you wouldn't say it to a man, don't say it to a woman. To get more specific in this skill, a generally great rule is to respond to all argumentative statements with generalized responses like, "Let me consider that." Probing questions to dive into the idea are also great. So long as people feel heard instead of shut down by your response, you're in the inclusiveness zone.

Language is a powerful signal of equity and inequity. Remember that language can be a weapon. You may be unintentionally shutting people down through power signaling with language. Aim to bring them up. Speak to everyone the same and communicate to signal that they are heard.

Keep the Sexy Stuff out of the Workplace

Apps and the Internet have changed the way we date. We can order a date as easily as we can toothpaste: express delivery within a few hours. The easiest way to avoid a #MeToo fail is to avoid sexual interest at work altogether. Self-manage away the tension and tingly feelings. If you take your job seriously and want to be taken seriously, you simply can't mix work with pleasure. There are subliminal ways your language and body cue sexuality when you communicate. If you are feeling the feels, your recipient can feel your vibes. If they don't like or want that—or, let's say, they want your job—you are simply taking on too much risk. As paradigms shift, we can all get caught more easily. I'm not allowed to feel butterflies for my attractive coworkers, and you aren't either.

Don't risk your entire career over any workplace interest. Close your eyes and imagine your future self, updating your LinkedIn profile and sending out resumes because your life has crumbled within your hands. You were crushing it and working so hard and then your damn sexy feelings got in the way. One beautiful intern showed up, and you made an inappropriate advance. You were justly fired, and that will follow you forever. Now you're fucked. It's not worth it.

You must take the universal approach because there are power imbalances invisible to you in the moment that you feel attracted to someone. It's easy to forget the business side when we get caught up in the human side. It's the power imbalance we don't even see that causes harassment. It was an unwanted advancement and they felt helpless to it. Not all advances are wanted and someone may retaliate. Treat office romance the same you would, say, smoking weed at your desk. Sure, you may get away with it, but there is a good chance you won't and it simply isn't worth the risk.

But beyond that? Don't be an asshole. Check your privilege. What you might consider innocent flirting may in fact be perceived as harassment by the other party. And never, ever, touch another person without their explicit permission, no matter how innocent it might seem to you. Ask first: Would you like a hug? Shake on it? High five? It's easy!

As an aside, I am friends with an army of very beautiful, smart women. We share stories for hours on end about different times that we were passed over for jobs, promotions, and projects. One woman even found an interoffice memo warning the men in the office of her "strong physical presence." If men weren't afraid of beautiful women in the workplace, you would have more productive teams and stronger leadership.

On top of that, let's examine beautiful people in general for a second. If you're motivated to keep to healthy wellness and fitness programs, then you're simply motivated. Human motivation transcends all areas of life, which is what I believe explains at least part of all the mounting research that shows attractive men are far more likely to get promotions and raises than their less attractive male peers.

Study after study shows a strong positive link between fitness and heightened cognitive function as well. It could be intelligence, it could be motivation, or some combination thereof, but attractive men are valuable assets in the workplace, so why wouldn't attractive women be as well? Stop being scared of us and start taking us seriously. You never know, maybe we'll just outperform. Don't be afraid.

KEY CONCEPTS

- People of all genders and identities contribute to issues and solutions; this is everyone's problem to tackle
- Make inclusion an open dialogue and part of your daily workplace rhetoric
- Learn to avoid gender-normative speaking: if you wouldn't say it to someone of the same gender, don't say it to a person of a different gender
- Ban sex and work completely: workplace sexuality needs boundaries

ASK YOURSELF

Remind yourself at work that this really is everyone's issue. In your next meeting ask yourself: "Am I being equal in my words to everyone in the room? Am I interrupting people? Am I exerting my power over a colleague for a gender-based reason? And above all else, am I flirting?" If so, stop.

12
Bonus

BECOME A KICK-ASS PUBLIC SPEAKER

You are not being judged, the value of what you are bringing to the audience is being judged. The topic of the talk isn't you, the topic of the talk is the audience, and specifically, how they can use your experience and knowledge to achieve their objectives.

—**SETH GODIN,** AUTHOR AND FORMER DOT-COM BUSINESS EXECUTIVE

Susan Cain did one of the bravest things any introvert could do: she gave a TED Talk. She stood on stage in front of thousands of people and millions of online viewers to share about the power of introverts and why introverts (I consider myself one) bring a lot of value to the table. This was a game changer for introverts in a lot of ways. Social norms shifted to be more forgiving. More importantly, what Susan Cain did for us was profound. If an introvert can do this, so can you.

Giving a TED Talk is the highest order of all great public speaking. People practice for years to give their TED Talk. There are codified formulas and flows to all of this. That's why I started this chapter with a quote from the greatest speaker of all time (in my and many others' opinion), Seth Godin. His online speaking resources are where I learned to go from being an awkward introvert to participating in a fairly impressive speaking circuit. I quote him throughout this chapter. Check out his online presentation skills for in-depth coverage on any topic listed.

PREPARE

Before we get into speaking techniques, let's talk preparedness. Prepare yourself for the ugly truth that people will probably remember only one thing from your presentation. Maybe, if you're compelling enough, they will remember three things. Decide what those one to three things are now and repeat them throughout your talk. This avoids letting people decide for themselves what those few key points are.

Practice this by writing down the key elements of your talk and then running an audit. If your talk starts bending the lines into other areas outside your key points, you need to either simplify it or expand it. As an example, I often see speakers give an emotional backstory to their childhood or an event of some sort, to create empathy with the audience. This is a perfect example of irrelevant diversion. Keep your anecdote on-message or get rid of it. For example, I once heard an incredibly compelling topic from an uncompelling speaker. He began his talk with a story of his wife's death. With the kindest of words, I had to explain afterward that while the story is important to him, it is not important to his talk or his audience. The talk itself is compelling enough. Let the talk be the talk.

Practice in Uncomfortable Settings

A lot of rookies make the mistake of mentally practicing instead of trying it aloud. Mentally practicing a talk is when you run through it in your head enough times to convince yourself that you are properly prepared to speak. With the best of intentions come the poorest of executions. Have you ever practiced this way, walked into an uncomfortable situation, and saw all of your words go out the window? The exact same thing happens in the professional speaking business. The words that come out are all that really matter. That's the part you'll need to practice.

Verbally practice. For your talk's sake, don't memorize it. Play with it over and over. Land your key points, but don't make it feel or look too rehearsed. Each time may be a bit different and that's perfectly okay. Record yourself giving the talk on video and study yourself after each take. It's not self-absorbed at all—actors do this all the time. I use the video recorder on my laptop. Expensive equipment isn't necessary.

When you finally feel comfortable with yourself, employ friends to give you feedback. Practicing in front of friends or family members is critical to prepare for onstage delivery. If you can do this without breaking into awkwardness, you can do the real thing, too.

Practice your talk *exactly* how you're going to deliver it. Find out the type of microphone, if any, and hold up a pencil as your handheld microphone in practice. Look around the empty room during your practices. The more you get comfortable prior to the actual event, the smoother the event will go. If you choose to write notecards, practice with them to confirm whether this is a good idea. I find myself staring down at my notecards to avoid eye contact, so I don't use them at all. You may want to hire a personal speaking or acting coach, although it is not necessary with enough effective practice.

Use Visuals as Your Highlight Reel

There is a lot of debate on whether you should use visuals while speaking publicly. Personally, I love them. They can act as your highlight reel for the points you wish to drive home.

I recognize that these are tough requirements, but there are creative ways of meeting them. A chart can be shown but should only include the words you need people to see. Erase the other stuff and make big, clear labels on the point of the chart.

Never include more than one idea per slide. Never include more than one sentence per slide. There's good logic to this. If people are reading, they aren't listening, meaning they aren't hearing you. If you want to show a narrative slide, stop and read it with everyone. That is the only time to bend the rule. Otherwise, keep slides with no words at all, or a few words at most.

Seth Godin says that "Slides are free." Cramming slides with information simply makes no sense. They're free. Use as many as you like. No more than one point—or better yet, one picture—per slide. One image can say more than a million words. It can represent the entire heart of the point you are trying to make. If at all possible, switch out words for an image.

Eye Contact

There is nothing worse than sitting through a talk in which the audience members are all on their cell phones. To be clear, unless there is world-changing news happening, this is 100 percent the speaker's own fault. It's a painful sight to watch. The speaker gets uncomfortable knowing that no one is listening, the talk gets worse, and the audience disconnects even further. I call this a toilet talk. Keeping attention through eye contact and all of the steps that follow should guarantee that you don't end up with a toilet talk.

As mentioned, you are in an arms race against technology. You must beat every cell phone in the room for undivided attention. Look at people directly as you speak. If eye contact is too uncomfortable, look right above their heads or practice the skill until you master it.

The general rule is to complete one sentence or one thought, making eye contact with one person. Then, move along the room smoothly from face-to-face and land another thought or idea on the next person. You don't need to individually connect. The point here is to make your presence known and let everyone know that you are watching them. Move all the way from one side of the room to the other, a bit randomly if you can, to keep everyone on their toes.

If you're working with cameras, treat them like people and be sure to connect with direct eye contact in the camera as well. Not too much, just a single thought or sentence, and then move along.

ABANDON YOUR SENSE OF CONTROL

At the SXSW Conference in 2018, a presenter stopped his presentation and demanded a new time slot because he had messed up his talk. He was trying to run video but it was slow and he had only awkward silence to fill the space. Not willing to accept this situation, he stopped the talk entirely and demanded that everyone come back tomorrow. He would figure out a new time slot with the directors to do the talk properly. I wasn't there; I just heard about it. Everybody heard about it. *Can you believe that guy?* Yes, I can. He's a control freak.

When you're giving a talk, you have to understand that you are not in control. Being a control freak will serve you well in other areas, if that's who you are, but not at a talk. This is about free-flowing commitment to your message. It's also about accepting the human and technological errors that can occur. A great speaker moves along seamlessly no matter what happens. They don't try to control the talk, they just keep it reeled in as best they can. This is done through practice. When you practice, you will screw up. When you screw up, you will recover. Screwing up is also part of your practice.

Connect with Humor, Stories, and Emotions

I recognize that these are professional-grade skills I'm giving you. It could be easy to overlook them if you are merely, say, presenting research findings to your team. Absolutely do not ignore these skills under any circumstances. Especially not the skill of emotionality. When it comes to business, emotions may make you feel uncomfortable. Let's take a step backward here to the ultimate goal. Your goal cannot be to bore everyone. Your goal cannot be to not be heard. Your goal must be to inspire people to action; otherwise, you're reading the wrong book.

Complicated matters need not be complicated. Find ways to make them simple. Break down ideas into how they actually relate to people, and revisit the discussion in chapter 3 about design thinking (page 21) to guide this further. The easiest way to translate your idea into a meaningful narrative is to think about how your idea affects people. The people listening, your customers, your family. Focus on the impact piece first, then tell a story that culminates with that impact.

What You Focus On

Standing out and inspiring others is about emotional connection. I work with a leading technologist at Pfizer to improve his speaking skills. He always begins with a story about his daughter's approach to technology. He tries explaining life before computing to his six-year-old daughter. Her response is, "But Daddy, if there were no computers, how did people download things from the Internet?" It wins over the crowd every time.

Here's another story from my work, to help you practice. We had a leader who wanted to give a resonant meeting with his entire staff. He wanted to inspire the team to do more, care more, and create better products. So instead of the usual format, where the speaker stands on stage and talks about quarterly earnings, we redesigned the impact of the meeting. Everything that was discussed was crafted in terms of the impact it had on customers. And you know what happened after the talk? Everyone was thinking and behaving differently, in terms of service to their customers. What people hear is what people focus on, if you can give them a compelling enough reason.

KEY CONCEPTS

- Prepare to speak about one to three big ideas
- Remember key concepts; do not memorize lines
- Physically prepare yourself for the real deal in every way possible
- Practice with friends and family members who make you feel awkward
- Eye contact and eye scanning prevents a disconnected audience

- Use slides as a highlight reel to amplify your story, not take away from it
- Aim for managing versus controlling your talk
- Connect with humor, stories, and emotions

ASK YOURSELF

When you are preparing for your next public speaking event, here are some key questions to run through: "Have I dedicated time to preparing this talk? Have I made it emotionally compelling? Have I practiced it at least five times out loud and to a friend?" Finally, examine every slide to be sure it has only one statement or one image. If not, break it out into more slides. Remember, "slides are free." Good luck!

Conclusion

Congratulations, you're now a master communicator!

Just kidding. The work has just begun. It's time to practice and hone your new skills. Learning to become a great communicator is like a bottomless pit, because the situations and contexts are constantly shifting around you, and there are always new ideas and audiences to learn and master. The point is, practice daily. Every day, find one trigger for you to practice your communication skills. It can be a stranger in a grocery store or a close relationship that you already have, like with your mother or a friend. Mindfully pause, select a strategy, and submit yourself to the process. It may feel a bit uncomfortable or unnatural at first, but practice and notice the results over time. As you begin achieving greater results from your communications, the skills will feel more natural to you.

The skills in this book have been organized into a series of 12 simple chapters, to make it easy for you to reference and use this book as you need, without having to revisit the entire narrative over again. Although the journey doesn't end here, you should be very proud of yourself for coming this far. If you are able to work on and put all these skills together, you will become an incredibly effective communicator.

FIVE WAYS TO STEP OUTSIDE YOUR COMFORT ZONE

I recently listened to a podcast with Tim Ferriss, who attributes his entire persona today to a time when he once stepped outside his own comfort zone. The truth is, he says, "We're all born naked and afraid." While many of our fears are designed to keep us alive, most of our fears are really quite irrational. We each own a set of limiting beliefs and expanding beliefs. The expanding beliefs tell us we can take an Uber to Mars. The limiting ones tell us we're too poor. You absolutely must start breaking through those limiting beliefs to succeed. And here are five ways you can do that now:

1. **List of worsts.** If there is something you want to do but are scared to try, write it down. Then, list the set of worst possible things that could happen. By simply writing these things down, it becomes pretty obvious that they aren't as rational as they sounded in your head.

2. **List of bests.** Write down the best possible things that could happen. Pretty compelling stuff happens in this list.

3. **Weigh your options.** If the bests list looks compelling and the worsts list doesn't include physical harm or death, it's worth it for you to do. Unleash your passion project.

4. **Start small.** Few people can run a marathon, but nearly anyone can run a city block. Break down the big feat into simple and achievable steps. Hack away at those, little by little, day by day.

5. **Visualize your future life.** Picture yourself completing your goal. Picture how you will feel. Imagine all the praise and admiration. Repeat this visualization in your head as you're slogging through the discomfort. Keep on, and that picture will be your reality.

Appendix
Communication Challenges and the Skills to Overcome Them

To help you master your communication skills, I've created the following chart to guide you in utilizing this book simply and to your advantage.

SITUATION	SKILLS TO USE	CHAPTERS
MEETING A NEW PERSON	Listen more than you speak Ask open questions Communicate with empathy Be respectful and inclusive	**1 3** **7 11**
COLLABORATING WITH A TEAM	Listen more than you speak Ask open questions Communicate with empathy Speak assertively Resolve conflict Be respectful and inclusive	**1 3 7** **9 11**
HANDLING A DIFFICULT COWORKER	Listen more than you speak Ask open questions Communicate with empathy Give constructive feedback Speak assertively Resolve conflict Be respectful and inclusive	**1 3 6** **7 9 11**

SITUATION	SKILLS TO USE	CHAPTERS
DELIVERING A BIG PRESENTATION	Present confident body language Utilize language psychology Speak assertively Resolve conflict Prepare for high-stakes communication with confidence Be respectful and inclusive Develop public speaking skills	**2 4 7** **10 11 12**
TAKING THE LEADERSHIP ROLE IN A MEETING OR PROJECT	Practice open listening Present confident body language Communicate with empathy Utilize language psychology Speak assertively Resolve conflict Prepare for high-stakes communication with confidence Be open and inclusive Develop public speaking skills	**1 2 3** **4 7 10** **11 12**
TRYING TO CLOSE A DEAL	Practice open listening Present confident body language Plan and communicate with empathy Utilize language psychology Be respectful and inclusive	**1 2 3** **4 11**

SITUATION	SKILLS TO USE	CHAPTERS
HIRING SOMEONE NEW	Listen more than you speak Ask open questions Study their body language communication Be respectful and inclusive	1 2 7 11
FIRING SOMEONE	Communicate with empathy Master delivering difficult feedback Be respectful and inclusive	3 6 11
ATTENDING A NETWORKING EVENT	Listen more than you speak Ask open questions Present confident body language Communicate with empathy Network your way into anything Be respectful and inclusive	1 2 3 5 11
INTERVIEWING FOR A JOB	Practice open listening Speak assertively Negotiate like a pro Be respectful and inclusive	1 7 8 11
TAKING THE STAGE AT A LARGE EVENT	Present confident body language Utilize language psychology Speak assertively Prepare for high-stakes communication with confidence Develop public speaking skills	2 4 9 10 12

Resources

Afremow, Jim. *The Champion's Mind: How Great Athletes Think, Train, and Thrive*. New York: Rodale Books, 2014. This book is for athletes, but it's also used by great leaders to up their mental games as well. A winning mind-set can be achieved—read this.

Carnegie, Dale. *How to Win Friends and Influence People*. New York: Pocket Books, 1998. This should be the first work of literature any expert points to on how to communicate. I've actually promised myself I'll relisten to the audiobook at least once a year. Please do so as well.

Cialdini, Robert B. *Influence: The Psychology of Persuasion*. New York: Harper Business, 2006. Robert Cialdini is the master of influential communication. His book has informed so many others, including mine, but the source material is transformational. Read it to learn the ins and outs of human influence.

Duckworth, Angela. *Grit: The Power of Passion and Perseverance*. New York: Scribner, 2016. Angela's research on how to succeed in business and life is simply amazing. A must-read for any curious mind that desires success.

Godin, Seth. *Whatcha Gonna Do with That Duck?* New York: Portfolio, 2012. Seth is simply the god of marketing and communication. Read all of his books and his blog, but start with this one.

Hsieh, Tony. *Delivering Happiness: A Path to Profits, Passion, and Purpose*. New York: Grand Central, 2013. Tony tells a beautiful narrative of his life, his work, and how to create a great business that can't be replicated. We use this as a case study for our clients on how a business can transform into a movement.

Moskowitz, Howard R. *Selling Blue Elephants: How to Make Great Products That People Want Before They Even Know They Want Them*. Upper Saddle River, NJ: Pearson Education, 2007. Howard's work was the baseline behind the millions of options we see in grocery stores today. His work is a transformational read for any marketer.

Nadella, Satya. *Hit Refresh: The Quest to Rediscover Microsoft's Soul and Imagine a Better Future for Everyone*. New York: HarperCollins, 2017. I love this book because it's a great example of how to transform an entire culture through empathy, listening, and, of course, communication.

Solis, Brian. "Once Upon a Digital Time: How to Be an Amazing Storyteller When Everyone is a 'Storyteller'." N.p.: LinkedIn, accessed April 30, 2018. https://business.linkedin.com /marketing-solutions/content-marketing/once-upon-a-digital -time-linkedin?trk=bl-po-ContentMarketing-20180328 -GapingVoid_NAMER&utm_source=blog&utm_medium =post&utm_campaign=LMS_LIT_20180328_GapingVoid _GLOBAL_NAMER_Blog&cid=7010d000001BnmfAAC. I am biasedly going to say that I absolutely adore this book our company created with Brian Solis. We break down the neuroscience of storytelling, along with the principles of marketing, to create a compelling and user-friendly read for any executive (as well as any average person).

References

Allworth, James. "Empathy: The Most Valuable Thing They Teach at HBS." *Harvard Business Review.* May 15, 2012. https://hbr .org/2012/05/empathy-the-most-valuable-thing-they-t.

Bernstein, Amy, Sarah Green Carmichael, and Nicole Torres. "Mind the (Wage) Gap." Produced by Amanda Kersey. *Women at Work* (podcast). *Harvard Business Review*, February 21, 2018. Audio, 44:09. https://hbr.org/podcast/2018/02/mind-the-wage-gap.

Bomey, Nathan. "Sexism in the Workplace Is Worse Than You Thought." *USA TODAY.* September 27, 2016. https://www .usatoday.com/story/money/2016/09/27/lean-in-study -women-in-the-workplace/91157026.

Bradberry, Travis. "Want to Hire People Who Are Emotionally Intelligent? Do These 5 Things." Ladders. April 22, 2018. https://www.theladders.com/career-advice/want-to-hire-people -who-are-emotionally-intelligent-do-these-5-things.

Carnegie, Dale. *How to Win Friends and Influence People.* New York: Pocket Books, 1998.

Cosmopolitan. "A Relationship Expert Answers 14 of Your Most Burning Dating Questions." *Cosmopolitan.* August 21, 2017. https://www.cosmopolitan.com/uk/love-sex/relationships/advice /g1179/matthew-hussey-answers-your-dating-relationship -questions.

Cuddy, Amy. "Your Body Language May Shape Who You Are." Filmed in June 2012 at TEDGlobal 2012. TED video, 20:56. https://www.ted.com/talks/amy_cuddy_your_body_language _shapes_who_you_are/transcript?language=en.

Davis, D. L. "Duffy on Track on Claim of 1,000-Seat Pickup by GOP since Obamacare." PolitiFact. July 27, 2017. http://www .politifact.com/wisconsin/statements/2017/jul/27/sean-duffy /duffy-track-claim-1000-seat-pickup-gop-obamacare.

Duckworth, Angela. *Grit: The Passion of Power and Perseverance.* New York: Scribner, 2016.

Folkman, Joseph. "The 6 Secrets of Successfully Assertive Leaders." *Forbes*. October 10, 2013. https://www.forbes.com/sites /joefolkman/2013/10/10/the-6-secrets-of-successfully -assertive-leaders/#2bcce3ce6668.

Godin, Seth. "Words on Slides." *SethGodin.com* (blog). April 6, 2018. http://sethgodin.typepad.com/seths_blog/2018/04/words-on -slides.html.

Golman, Russell, and George Loewenstein. *An Information-Gap Theory of Feelings About Uncertainty.* Pittsburgh, PA: Carnegie Mellon University, 2016. https://www.cmu.edu/dietrich/sds/docs /golman/Information-Gap%20Theory%202016.pdf.

Goman, Carol Kinsey. "The Body Language of Women Running for President." *Forbes*. October 29, 2015. https://www.forbes.com /sites/carolkinseygoman/2015/10/29/fiorina-vs-clinton-whose -body-language-would-win/#2a43f433119f.

Gray, Patrick. "The Lie of Multitasking." TechRepublic. August 13, 2013. https://www.techrepublic.com/blog/tech-decision-maker /the-lie-of-multitasking.

Hess, Abigail. "Study: Using Emojis in a Work Email Makes You Seem Incompetent." CNBC.com. August 25, 2017. https://www.cnbc .com/2017/08/24/study-using-emojis-in-a-work-email-makes -you-seem-incompetent.html.

Higgins, Jessica. "How to Finally Stop Sexual Harassment at Work." *Entrepreneur*. April 16, 2018. https://www.entrepreneur.com /article/311587.

Koza, Jennifer. "5 Disturbing Sexual Harassment Statistics We Can't Afford to Ignore." Fairygodboss.com. Accessed April 30, 2018. https://fairygodboss.com/articles/sexual-harassment-statistics.

Laing, Karen. "How Your Physical Health Controls Your Mental Success." *The Guardian.* February 4, 2016. https://www .theguardian.com/women-in-leadership/2016/feb/04/how -your-physical-health-controls-your-mental-success.

Larson, Jeffry H. *The Great Marriage Tune-Up Book: A Proven Program for Evaluating and Renewing Your Relationship.* San Francisco: Jossey-Bass, 2003.

Lee, S., and M. S. Crockett. "Effect of Assertiveness Training on Levels of Stress and Assertiveness Experienced by Nurses in Taiwan, Republic of China." *Issues in Mental Health Nursing* 15, no. 4 (1994): 419–432. https://www.ncbi.nlm.nih.gov/pubmed /8056571.

Liu, Yichuan, Elise A. Piazza, Erez Simony, Patricia A. Shewokis, Banu Onaral, Uri Hasson, and Hasan Ayaz. "Measuring Speaker– Listener Neural Coupling with Functional Near Infrared Spectroscopy." *Scientific Reports* 7 (2017). doi:10.1038/ srep43293.

McKay, Brett, and Kate McKay. "Quit Being a Pushover: How to Be Assertive." *The Art of Manliness* (blog). Last modified March 22, 2018. https://www.artofmanliness.com/articles/how-to -be-assertive.

Microsoft News Center. "Satya Nadella Email to Employees on First Day as CEO." Microsoft.com. February 4, 2014. https://news .microsoft.com/2014/02/04/satya-nadella-email-to-employees -on-first-day-as-ceo.

Noland, Marcus, and Tyler Moran. "Study: Firms with More Women in the C-Suite Are More Profitable." *Harvard Business Review.* February 8, 2016. https://hbr.org/2016/02/study-firms-with-more -women-in-the-c-suite-are-more-profitable.

Pease, Allan, and Barbara Pease. *The Definitive Book of Body Language*. New York: Bantam Dell, 2004.

Peck, Emily. "The Lack of Women Leaders Is a National Emergency." *Huffington Post*. October 28, 2017. https://www.huffingtonpost.com/entry/women-leadership-sexual-harassment_us_59f387cae4b03cd20b818ed1.

Purtill, Corinne. "Researchers Have Isolated Exactly How to Make Conflict in Relationships Healthy." *Quartz*. January 28, 2016. https://qz.com/604287/researchers-have-isolated-exactly-how-to-make-conflict-in-relationships-healthy/.

Raz, Guy. "Tim Ferriss: How Can We Become Comfortable with Discomfort?" *TED Radio Hour* (podcast). NPR, April 27, 2018. Audio, 12:27. https://www.npr.org/2018/04/27/606078336/tim-ferriss-how-can-we-become-comfortable-with-discomfort.

Sankar, Carol. "How the '5 Second Rule' Can Help You Fight the Urge to Procrastinate." *Inc*. December 8, 2017. https://www.inc.com/carol-sankar/how-to-kick-habit-of-procrastination-in-5-seconds-according-to-a-bestselling-author-top-speaker.html.

Solomon, Micah. "8 Ways to Improve Patient Satisfaction, Patient Experience and (by the Way) HCAHPS Scores." *Forbes*. January 11, 2015. https://www.forbes.com/sites/micahsolomon/2015/01/11/8-ways-to-improve-patient-satisfaction-and-patient-experience-and-by-the-way-improve-hcahps-scores/#2bd9b5965191.

Stanger, Melissa. "Attractive People Are Simply More Successful." *Business Insider*. October 9, 2012. http://www.businessinsider.com/attractive-people-are-more-successful-2012-9.

Vanderkam, Laura. "Why Managers Should Spend Exactly 6 Hours a Week with Each Employee." *Fast Company*. July 14, 2014. https://www.fastcompany.com/3032972/why-managers-should-spend-exactly-6-hours-a-week-with-each-employee.

Waytz, Adam. "The Limits of Empathy." *Harvard Business Review*. Accessed April 30, 2018. https://hbr.org/2016/01/the-limits -of-empathy.

Zak, Paul J. "Why Inspiring Stories Make Us React: The Neuroscience of Narrative." *Cerebrum* (2015): 2. https://www.ncbi.nlm.nih.gov /pmc/articles/PMC4445577.

Zak, Paul J. "Why Your Brain Loves Good Storytelling." *Harvard Business Review*. October 28, 2014. https://hbr.org/2014/10 /why-your-brain-loves-good-storytelling.

Zenger, Jack, and Joseph Folkman. "What Great Listeners Actually Do." *Harvard Business Review*. July 14, 2016. https://hbr.org /2016/07/what-great-listeners-actually-do.

Index

A

active listening, 5
Amazon, 39, 64
Apple, 72
assertiveness
    assertive statements in conflict situations, 73
    communicating to the yes, 57
    defining, 56
    good intent, assuming, 60, 62
    practice of, 58–59, 60
    as a skill to use, 61, 107–109
    superhero stance, aiding in assertive attitude, 13
    turning assertiveness on and off, 11
attractiveness factor in success, 94
authentic caring, 60, 76, 84–85, 87

B

Ballmer, Steve, 1
Banks, Tyra, 48
Bezos, Jeff, 64
biases, 3, 5, 27, 92
body language
    in conflict resolution, 75
    facial expressions, 5, 9, 14, 17, 76
    mimicry, 14–15, 16
    power stances, 12–13, 17
    in presidential election, 11
    as a skill to use, 108–109
break-even point, 58
Bridgewater Associates, 47
bullying tactics, 75–77, 79
business cards, 41, 42, 43

C

Cain, Susan, 96
Carnegie, Dale, 75, 78, 110
Cialdini, Robert, 21, 110
comfort zone, 50, 58, 105–106
communication brain errors, 30–33
conflict
    as an opportunity, 72, 79
    bullying tactics, 76–77, 79
    common interests, aligning, 74–75, 79
    conflict resolution as a skill to use, 107–108
    e-mail, avoiding use of in conflict resolution, 75, 79
    right intentions, 78
contextual interference, 67, 70
credibility, 84, 87
criticism, 11, 47, 50–53
Cuddy, Amy, 13

D

design thinking, 21, 100
Duckworth, Angela, 86, 110

T

triggers, 3, 43, 58, 105

V

visualization, 83, 106

W

walk point, setting, 66, 70

wearables, 4

winner's mind-set, 83, 87

winner's V, 12

Woman Interrupted app, 91

Z

Zappos, 39

About the Author

JESSICA HIGGINS, JD, MBA, BB, is a public speaker, strategic consultant, and published author in the field of organizational culture design. She serves as the chief operating officer of Gapingvoid Culture Design Group, where she and her team design and shift culture through management science, communication change, behavior design, and influence. Clients include Microsoft, Zappos, AT&T, Pfizer, L'Oréal, U.S. Bank, Babson College, and many others. She also holds board advisory positions in arts and technology organizations.

She holds a black belt in Lean Six Sigma, a juris doctor in law, a master's in business management, and a bachelor's degree in behavioral psychology and has studied under Professor BJ Fogg in the area of behavioral design.

She has been an equality advocate for more than 15 years, serving as president of the Texas Pay Equity Committee when she was 19 years old, becoming a female executive in her company at the age of 26, and founding her own firm by the age of 29. She is frequently interviewed and published on female entrepreneurship, millennial workforces, and gender and equality issues. She advises and mentors women in business success and leadership skills.

Jessica's personal accounts from this book came from her work as chief operating officer of a consulting firm. Jessica now owns Digital Unicorns, an agency that helps individuals and companies communicate more effectively to market themselves and their businesses. Visit Digital-Unicorns.com for more information.

For more information about the author,
visit her website at JessicaHiggins.co.

CPSIA information can be obtained
at www.ICGtesting.com
Printed in the USA
JSHW031746200221
11953JS00002B/39